FRANCIS FRITH'S

LANCASTER - A HISTORY AND CELEBRATION

THE FRANCIS FRITH COLLECTION

www.francisfrith.com

LANCASTER

A HISTORY & CELEBRATION

ROBERT SWAIN

THE FRANCIS FRITH COLLECTION

www.francisfrith.com

First published in the United Kingdom in 2004
by The Francis Frith Collection®

Hardback edition 2004 ISBN 1-90493-834-5
Paperback edition 2012 ISBN 978-1-84589-642-3

British Library Cataloguing in Publication Data

Lancaster - A History & Celebration
Robert Swain

The Francis Frith Collection®
Oakley Business Park, Wylye Road,
Dinton, Wiltshire SP3 5EU
Tel: +44 (0) 1722 716 376
Email: info@francisfrith.co.uk
www.francisfrith.com

Printed and bound in Great Britain
Contains material sourced from responsibly managed forests

Front Cover: **LANCASTER, THE TOWN HALL 1912** 64215t

Additional modern photographs by Robert Swain.

Domesday extract used in timeline by kind permission of
Alecto Historical Editions, www.domesdaybook.org
Aerial photographs reproduced under licence from
Simmons Aerofilms Limited.
Historical Ordnance Survey maps reproduced under licence from
Homecheck.co.uk

Every attempt has been made to contact copyright holders of
illustrative material. We will be happy to give full acknowledgement in future editions
for any items not credited. Any information should be directed to The Francis Frith
Collection.

*The colour-tinting in this book is for illustrative purposes only,
and is not intended to be historically accurate*

AS WITH ANY HISTORICAL DATABASE, THE FRANCIS FRITH ARCHIVE IS
CONSTANTLY BEING CORRECTED AND IMPROVED, AND THE PUBLISHERS WOULD
WELCOME INFORMATION ON OMISSIONS OR INACCURACIES

CONTENTS

LANCASTER FROM THE AIR 1929   AF26404

A HISTORY & CELEBRATION

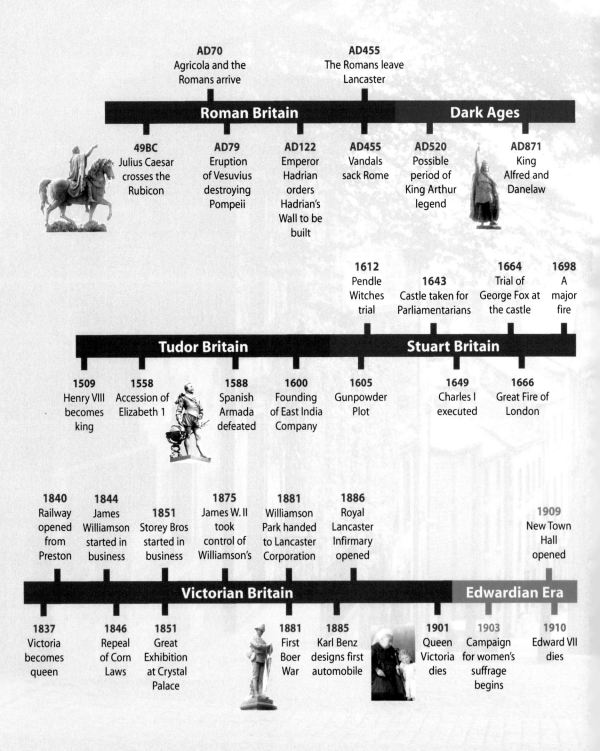

AD70
Agricola and the Romans arrive

AD455
The Romans leave Lancaster

Roman Britain

Dark Ages

49BC
Julius Caesar crosses the Rubicon

AD79
Eruption of Vesuvius destroying Pompeii

AD122
Emperor Hadrian orders Hadrian's Wall to be built

AD455
Vandals sack Rome

AD520
Possible period of King Arthur legend

AD871
King Alfred and Danelaw

1612
Pendle Witches trial

1643
Castle taken for Parliamentarians

1664
Trial of George Fox at the castle

1698
A major fire

Tudor Britain

Stuart Britain

1509
Henry VIII becomes king

1558
Accession of Elizabeth 1

1588
Spanish Armada defeated

1600
Founding of East India Company

1605
Gunpowder Plot

1649
Charles I executed

1666
Great Fire of London

1840
Railway opened from Preston

1844
James Williamson started in business

1851
Storey Bros started in business

1875
James W. II took control of Williamson's

1881
Williamson Park handed to Lancaster Corporation

1886
Royal Lancaster Infirmary opened

1909
New Town Hall opened

Victorian Britain

Edwardian Era

1837
Victoria becomes queen

1846
Repeal of Corn Laws

1851
Great Exhibition at Crystal Palace

1881
First Boer War

1885
Karl Benz designs first automobile

1901
Queen Victoria dies

1903
Campaign for women's suffrage begins

1910
Edward VII dies

HISTORICAL TIMELINE FOR LANCASTER

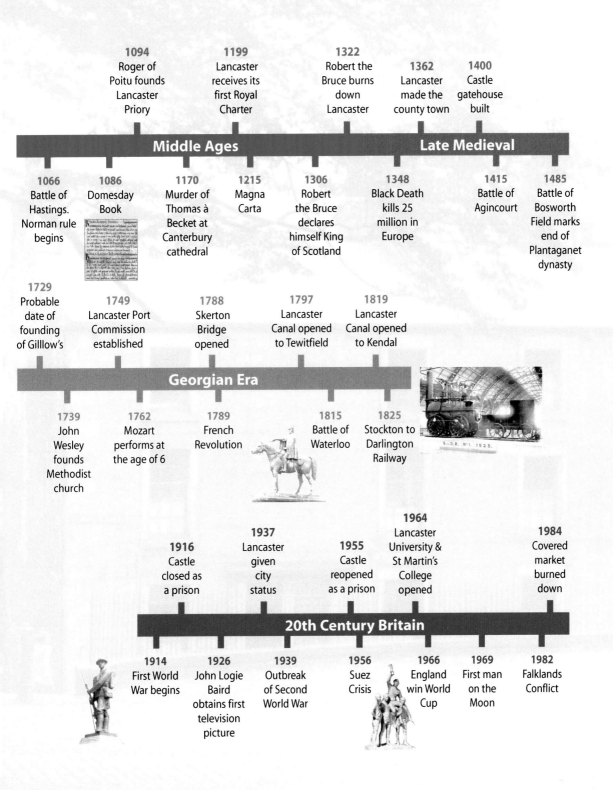

1094 Roger of Poitu founds Lancaster Priory

1199 Lancaster receives its first Royal Charter

1322 Robert the Bruce burns down Lancaster

1362 Lancaster made the county town

1400 Castle gatehouse built

Middle Ages

Late Medieval

1066 Battle of Hastings. Norman rule begins

1086 Domesday Book

1170 Murder of Thomas à Becket at Canterbury cathedral

1215 Magna Carta

1306 Robert the Bruce declares himself King of Scotland

1348 Black Death kills 25 million in Europe

1415 Battle of Agincourt

1485 Battle of Bosworth Field marks end of Plantaganet dynasty

1729 Probable date of founding of Gillow's

1749 Lancaster Port Commission established

1788 Skerton Bridge opened

1797 Lancaster Canal opened to Tewitfield

1819 Lancaster Canal opened to Kendal

Georgian Era

1739 John Wesley founds Methodist church

1762 Mozart performs at the age of 6

1789 French Revolution

1815 Battle of Waterloo

1825 Stockton to Darlington Railway

1964 Lancaster University & St Martin's College opened

1984 Covered market burned down

1916 Castle closed as a prison

1937 Lancaster given city status

1955 Castle reopened as a prison

20th Century Britain

1914 First World War begins

1926 John Logie Baird obtains first television picture

1939 Outbreak of Second World War

1956 Suez Crisis

1966 England win World Cup

1969 First man on the Moon

1982 Falklands Conflict

CHAPTER ONE

SETTING THE SCENE

LANCASTER HAS a long and rich history. That history is mainly about people: those who visited and those who stayed, those in business and commerce and those who laboured in businesses, honest and upright people and people who committed a variety of crimes, those who came to learn and those who came to teach. This book looks at a few of those people.

Some of the first people to visit Lancaster were the Romans. It was about AD70 when the first Roman commander would have looked out on the scene from the top of the hill where the castle now stands. Over the following years, he and his successors would see change to the town; the Roman fort would be built, and no doubt there are more remains of Roman buildings now hidden underground below the priory church and nearby. Below, near where the bus station stands, he would see the Roman ships at the port on the River Lune, which then followed a different course.

The Roman fort was not a major fort, but an auxiliary one; it was built on a drumlin, or ridge, left by a retreating glacier at the end of the last ice age, and stood above the lowest crossing point of the River Lune. One place where the river may have been crossed at that time is Scale Ford, below Carlisle Bridge; the other would be somewhere near the Millennium Bridge or Greyhound Bridge. The Roman name of the fort is not known, but the name Lancaster itself is derived from the river name, 'Lune' or 'Loyne', and 'castrum', the Roman for 'camp'.

THE VIEW FROM THE CASTLE 1927 80504

If he left his fort by the east gate, the Roman commander would pass through the gate and follow the road down what is Church Street today, which in his day was the 'vicus' or civilian settlement. There, he and his men would be able to trade with the local people. At the end of that road he would be able to turn right along another road, now Cheapside, formerly Pudding Lane and Butchers Lane. At the end of the road there would probably be a wall, and beyond it he would see the graveyard - the Romans buried their dead outside town walls. Various artefacts have been found here during archaeological digs over the years.

By the end of the Romans' time here, Lancaster had become Christian, and it is believed that there was a church around where St Mary's Church, the priory church, now stands. Beyond the present church are the remains of the Roman bath-house (L10701k, below), which are still to be seen in the field to the right when walking from the castle past the church and down to the river. To the left, the shape of the land shows that it was part of the old fort - three were built on the site over the years.

THE REMAINS OF A ROMAN BATH-HOUSE NEAR THE PRIORY CHURCH 2004 L10701k (Robert Swain)

After the Romans departed, local people no doubt continued to live in the town, but there is not much information about them. It was not until the 7th century that the Anglo-Saxons, principally the Anglians, arrived in Lancaster in any number; by this time they were largely Christian. The town became a part of Northumbria, for a time the most powerful of the kingdoms in the country as a whole. They built a church here; a Saxon doorway and crosses have been found.

The Angles were well settled and had intermarried with the Romano-British locals by the time the Vikings came to the area. Some of the Vikings came over from the east – the evidence for this is place names ending in '-by', such as Hornby – but most would be Norsemen who came down the west coast from Orkney and Shetland, the Isle of Man and Ireland, and they were to settle as

EDENBRECK

This scene looking across to the castle and the priory was taken from one of the ancient fields of Lancaster, named Edenbreck by the Norse. The public footpaths of today are often old routes connecting farms together. From Edenbreck, one path goes to Carr House, another old farm in the town, and the other across to the old entrance to Aldcliffe Hall and its adjoining farmland. Edenbreck farm would have been at the edge of Lancaster in Norse times.

DISTANT VIEW 1891 28596

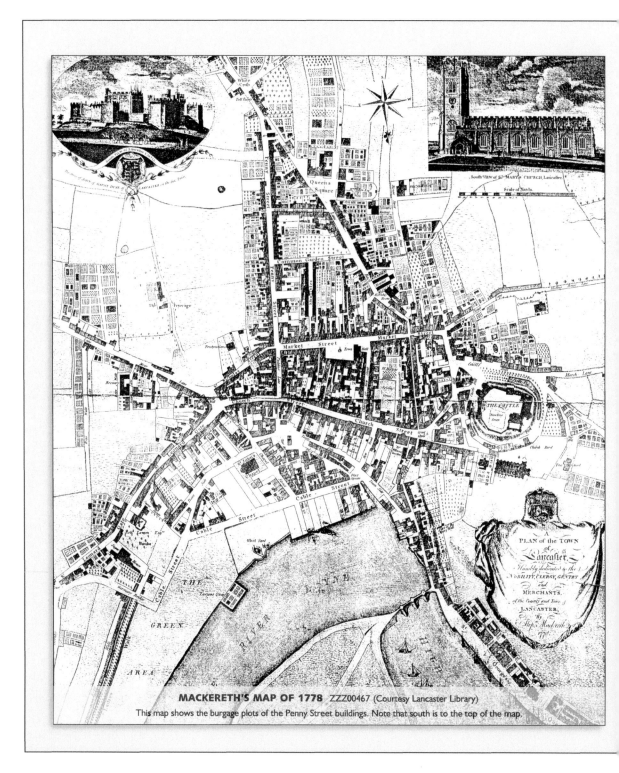

MACKERETH'S MAP OF 1778 ZZZ00467 (Courtesy Lancaster Library)
This map shows the burgage plots of the Penny Street buildings. Note that south is to the top of the map.

BURGAGE PLOTS

PENNY STREET c1950 LI0004

The main houses lining Lancaster's streets in medieval times each had their own strip of land, known as burgage plots. (The word 'burgage' relates to tenures of land in towns held for the king or another lord.) Sometimes there were passageways between the plots. This can still be seen in Penny Street, where the plots go back to Mary Street, with an ancient passage remaining as a right of way by the Halifax. There were once attempts made to close the passage, but a Lancaster businessman fought for its retention.

farmers. They gave the name '-dale' to the valleys, such as Lonsdale or Lunesdale. Norse names still endure in some Lancaster fields that are now parts of estates, such as Haverbreaks and Edenbreck (see 28596, on page 13 - Edenbreck was a farm for a long time). Both of these names are partly derived from 'brekka', the Norse for 'hill'.

Around Lancaster the Vikings mixed with the Anglo-Saxons, rather than taking over their land as conquerors. Whilst he was probably hardly seen in the town, if at all, the Saxon Earl Tostig held much land in what are now north Lancashire and south Cumbria; his seat was in Halton. Harold Godwinson of Wessex, his brother, killed Tostig, who was a traitor, at the Battle of Stamford Bridge in 1066. In turn Harold went on to be killed at the Battle of Hastings a few days later, having being crowned King of England in defiance of a pledge of the crown to William, Duke of Normandy.

A NORMAN SHIP F6019

Now it was the turn of the Normans to come to Lancaster and take control of the whole area. (They were originally another branch of the Vikings, who had settled in Normandy.) A rising by the English in Yorkshire was crushed, and the lands laid waste. The Normans

THE CASTLE GATEWAY 1896 37369

compiled the Domesday Book, a survey of England for taxation purposes, in 1066: in it Lancaster is listed in two parts, Lancaster and Church Lancaster. It was the Normans who made the Forest of Bowland a royal forest or hunting ground, and subject to very strict forest laws.

Roger of Poitu, a relative of William the Conqueror, was given lands covering most of Lancashire, and around 1093 he built himself a stone castle, no trace of which survives. In 1094 he founded the priory on the hill by the old Roman fort. Monks came over from his home town of Seez in Normandy to run it.

Because Roger was granted his estates, which were known as the Honour of Lancaster, directly from King William Rufus, he was a very powerful man, and he held his own court to dispense justice at least once a year. At those courts, the freeholders of his manors could not sit, but had to stand bareheaded. It was at this time that the county of Lancashire was formed, and Lancaster became the county town.

In 1199 Lancaster received its first royal charter from King John. This changed what had been a village to a borough, and gave Lancaster some special privileges, including permission to take wood from the forest of Quernmore for building; it also gave the burgesses the right to graze their animals in the forest as far from the town as they could return home within the day.

One group of visitors who were not welcome in Lancaster were the Scots: in 1322, King Robert the Bruce's army burned down the timber houses of the town, leaving only the two religious buildings untouched. These were the priory and the Dominican friary. The Dominicans were known as 'black friars', and their friary was where Sulyard Street now stands. No mention is made of what happened to the stone-built castle, but it was probably left alone. After the Bruce's visit, the town had to be rebuilt.

Lancaster Castle was, in theory, the residence of the lord of the Honour of Lancaster. Only parts of the old building remain: the principal features are the Norman keep and the much altered Adrian's Tower (also known as Hadrian's Tower). John o'Gaunt's son, the future Henry IV, built the impressive gatehouse around 1400 (see page 16), and to a large extent it took over the role of the

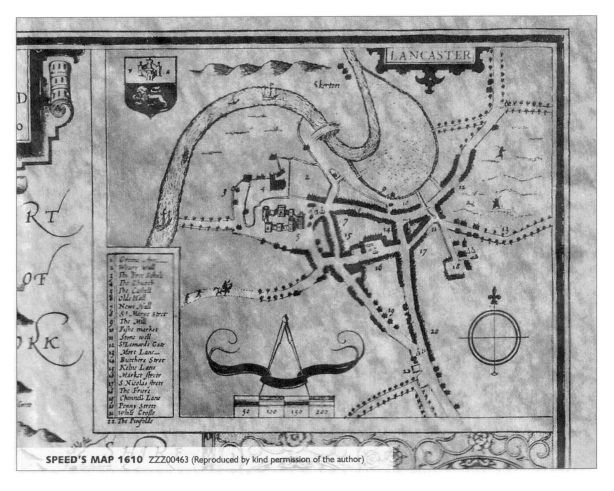

SPEED'S MAP 1610 ZZZ00463 (Reproduced by kind permission of the author)

MARKET SQUARE c1955 L10049p

The old market square at this time was occupied by
bus shelters, and beside them are the steps leading
down to the underground public lavatories - these
were buried when the area was pedestrianised.
Bradleys was a well-known outfitters at that time.

keep. It is still the main entrance. It was Henry's estates that became the Duchy of Lancaster, which have belonged to the Crown ever since.

John o' Gaunt visited Lancaster in 1385 and 1393 for a total of nine days, and they were the only times he came here in his life. It is very unlikely that his horse cast the original of the shoe in the pavement at Horse Shoe Corner – the shoe is more likely to have originally announced the coming of a horse fair. Henry, John o'Gaunt's son, did stay in Lancaster for a while in 1409.

In spite of the town being so little visited by royalty, in 1362 Lancaster was made the seat of the assizes and the 'Principal Town of the said County', and so it assumed its judicial importance that continues today; courts are still held in the castle.

1414 saw Henry V hand over the priory to trustees, who gave it to the Bridgettine Convent of Syon, owing to Henry's dislike of the monastery revenues going overseas. It was not until 1430, on the death of Prior Giles Lovell, that the convent was able to take possession of the church; it then became the parish church of the town, which saved it from destruction at the time of the Reformation, unlike the friary. The area for which it was responsible was wide: in 1650 it included not only Lancaster but Fulwood near Preston, Wyresdale, Admarsh, Overton, Toxteth, Stalmine, Gressingham, and Caton. Later, Bleasdale and Poulton (Morecambe) were added and Toxteth removed.

Market Square is shown on Speed's map of 1610 (page 17), the first real map of the town. The cross would have stood on the site of the present fountain. Close by was the pillory, where wrongdoers were imprisoned and people were able to throw things at them, such as rotten eggs. Originally the square would include New Street Square; however, the original Town Hall of the 14th century already encroached into the square. The market would be a busy place with the various stalls; the fish stalls at that time stood on what is now Damside Street.

A MEDIEVAL KNIGHT AND HIS LADY F6018

PENNY STREET c1950 L10004

CHAPTER TWO

TRIALS, TROUBLES
AND TRADES

THOMAS COVELL is locally remembered by the stone Covell Cross, standing at the head of Church Street (which used to be St Marygate). Although it is called Covell Cross, and stands on the site of a medieval cross, it was erected to celebrate the coronation of Edward VII. Covell must have been an important and well-respected Lancaster man, although little is now known about him. He was mayor of Lancaster six times, a justice of the peace, and a coroner, and also the keeper of the prison at Lancaster Castle for forty-eight years. Thomas Covell built a stone house for himself in the 1630s; this is now known as The Judge's Lodgings at the top of Church Street, and just below the Castle. It was built on the site of an earlier house.

Supposedly Covell was both anti-witch and anti-Catholic, but his daughter was to marry a member of the strongly Catholic Brockholes family, and it is said that a number of Catholics 'escaped' from the castle during his time. There are contrasting stories about how he treated prisoners, which vary from his being very lenient and allowing some Roman Catholics to escape, to being cold and inattentive to their conditions. Covell was a rich man, leaving over £3,000 when he died in 1639, a very large sum for those days. There is a memorial brass to him in the priory church.

Covell would see a notorious group of prisoners brought to the Castle in 1612: these were the Pendle Witches, a total of 14 women and five men from the Pendle area in east Lancashire. The times of James I were ones of anti-popery, when the people were expected to follow the religion of their king. However, Lancashire was a strongly Roman Catholic area. This was also a time when so-called witches (who tended to live in poorer areas) were persecuted; the king believed very strongly in their evil powers. Both these factors came into account in this case.

Two very old and ugly women lived around Pendle, Elizabeth Southern or Southernes and Anne Whittle, 'Old Demdike' and 'Old Chattox' respectively. The fact that they were both about 80 years old at a time when people did not live as long as they do now would go against them. The two were in business selling spells, cures and charms, which was regarded by some as a threat to the Christian Church. Also, they had strong influences over their respective families. In April 1612 Demdike and Chattox, together with Alizon Device and Anne Redfern, were brought through the Trough of Bowland to Lancaster for trial.

Their friends and families then met on Good Friday 1612, when, it was alleged, they planned the destruction of the castle and the murder of Covell before the next assize court. Other witches were then found around the Forest of Pendle and also brought to Lancaster for 'justice'. Whilst some of those involved may well have believed themselves to be witches, the evidence against them would not have stood up to investigation in modern times, that given by Jennet Device, Demdike's nine-year-old granddaughter, being particularly dubious. Some of the charges against the witches related to the deaths of children, but this was a time of disease and high infant mortality.

In some ways Old Demdike was the luckiest

of the witches, as she died in the castle dungeons before her case came to be heard. Eight women and two men were found guilty and sentenced to death at the August 1612 Assize Court. No doubt Covell saw them before they were taken out of the castle jail to Lancaster Moor, where they were hanged before a crowd of onlookers.

Following on from the Reformation in 1536 and the Pilgrimage of Grace, Roman Catholics were severely persecuted. There then followed the most gruesome period in Lancaster's history, when many Catholics, especially priests, were tried and then sentenced to death on the Moor. Many of these religious martyrs, who died for their faith, were hanged, drawn and quartered, a most horrible death.

Lancaster itself did not particularly take sides during the Civil Wars, but the town was of strategic importance with its castle and also its position on a major north-south route, together with the crossing of the Lune. It also had great symbolic value as the county town. It is odd that although there were Royalist supporters further up the Lune valley, neither the castle nor the town were garrisoned by them in 1642. As a result, in February 1643 a company under sergeant-major Birch came up from Preston and took the surrender of the castle for the Parliamentarians.

This was not the end of the Royalist cause. The Earl of Derby then decided it was important that his forces should retake Lancaster; he set out from Wigan on 13 March, possibly having decided to do so because of the wreck of a Spanish vessel off Rossall Point in the Fylde - its 22 cannon had been taken to Lancaster Castle. On the way to Lancaster he added to his numbers by gaining troops from the Fylde. He arrived on 18 March, entering the 'Towne of Lancaster several waies' and meeting very little resistance, for the Parliamentary troops had retreated into the security of the castle. As a result, the town was open to plunder and burning. Penny Street in particular suffered, its timber and thatch buildings soon being set ablaze, the garrison having abandoned them to their fate. It is estimated that ninety premises were lost; in 1645 Parliament made a grant of £8,000 as compensation for them, but with strings attached. Later in the war, a 'rude company of Yorkshire Troopers', whom even the Parliamentarians admitted were a problem, garrisoned the castle.

At the end of the first phase of the Civil War, Charles I was executed in January 1649. In 1651 his son invaded the country, coming down from Scotland. It would be very crowded in Market Square on 11 August that year when Charles II was proclaimed king at the Market Cross. He spent the night at Ashton Hall. Before leaving the town he had ordered that the gates of the castle be opened and the prisoners released. However, the monarchy was not actually restored until 1660.

At the end of the Civil War it was decided to demolish the castle so that it could not be garrisoned, but to retain those parts used for the courts and the prison. This left the gatehouse and the buildings on the south and west sides. The levelling of the ground on the east side had the odd effect of putting some of

Fact File

At the top of Lungess Tower or the keep of the castle is 'John o'Gaunt's Chair', which rises a further 10 feet higher. This was the beacon tower of the castle, which was used both for warning beacons and celebratory ones, such as for coronations. At the time of the approach of the Spanish Armada, the beacon on 'Gaunt's embattled pile' was seen on Skiddaw in the Lake District, warning of the danger to England.

the windows of Covell's house below ground level. Much damage must have been done to the castle, for it was estimated that repairs would cost nearly £2,000 when a return to military usage was proposed in 1664.

George Fox, the founder of the Quaker movement, came to Lancaster and preached in 1652. At the Sessions before Justice Sawrey and Justice Thompson, about forty priests appeared against Fox. With the support of Judge Fell, the hearing turned into a triumph for Fox and his preaching. Things were

different when Fox was brought back to the sessions in 1664 for refusing to take the oath of allegiance (after the restoration of the Stuart monarchy, everybody was supposed to swear allegiance to the king and the Church of England). He was kept until the Assizes and appeared before Judge Twisden. Fox wore his hat when appearing in court instead of removing it in deference to the judge, much to Twisden's annoyance. Following Fox's refusal to take off his hat, a jailer removed it. During the argument with the judge which followed, Fox explained that he had never taken an oath in his life, and that to do so was against the teachings of Christ. Two days later he again appeared before the judge, who did not then make as much of him wearing his hat. Fox was then committed until the following Assizes.

During his trial before Judge Turner at those Assizes, Fox spoke for himself, saying that he had much to say if the judge would have the patience to listen. The judge and others were amused at this, and asked what he could have to say. Fox then asked if the oath was tendered to the king's subjects or to foreign princes. The judge said that it was to 'the subjects of this realm'. Fox then pointed out that on his indictment the word 'subject' had been omitted, so that he could not be judged for that. The judge confessed that it was an error.

Fox then went on to point out that there was something else to stop his trial, and asked Turner to look at what day the indictment was tendered to him at the Sessions. Turner and the court officials looked and replied that it was on the eleventh of January. Fox then asked on what day of the week the Sessions were held, and was told that they were held on a Tuesday. He then told the judge and justices to look at their almanacs, and they would see that the eleventh of January was a Monday. Fox went on to say: 'ye have indicted me for refusing the oath in the Quarter Sessions held at Lancaster on the eleventh day of January last, and the Justices have sworn that they tendered the oath in open Sessions here that day, and the jury upon their oaths have found me guilty thereupon; and yet ye see there were no Sessions held in Lancaster that day'. At this, the justices flew into a rage.

After that, Fox went on to ask when the last Assize court was held, and the judge said that it was the sixteenth year of the king. Fox then pointed out that the indictment said that it was in the fifteenth year. The justices were then all 'in a fret again' at the error, the judge having sworn to the officers of the Court that the oath had been tendered to him at the Assize mentioned in the indictment. Fox then went on to show that parts of the oath were missing from the indictment, although it should all have been included.

In the end, the judge decided that Fox was free from the charges against him, but then told him that he would have to take the oath there and then. A bible was produced, but rather than take the oath, Fox showed that the Bible said 'Swear not at all'. Fox asked why he was to be imprisoned for doing as the Bible said, but nobody, including priests present, answered the question. Further discussion on the indictment took place,

and Fox was committed to prison until the following Assizes.

The prison part of the castle must have been in poor condition as well as the military part. The evidence for this is George Fox's description of it during his imprisonment in 1664. He was put into a tower where the smoke of the other rooms came up so thick as to stand like dew on the walls; sometimes the haze was so great that he could hardly see his own burning candle. The under-jailer could hardly be persuaded to come up to unlock one of the upper doors above him when the smoke was thick, owing to his own fear of it. Rain fell upon Fox's bed, and when he tried to stop it in the winter his shift would be 'as wet as muck with the rain that came in upon me'. Where he was held was high, so that as fast as he stopped up the hole, the wind would blow it out again. Fox lay in these conditions all winter until the next Assize Court. As this description does not match any of the present building, it is thought that Fox was held in a tower that has now been demolished.

George Fox was brought before the following Assize Court, where he once more showed that the word 'subject' was missing again in the indictment. The judge then ordered him to be taken away, and did not give him the chance to show other errors in the indictment. Fox never again appeared before the Lancaster Assize Court, but was taken to Scarborough and imprisoned there. Other Quaker prisoners of conscience were held at Lancaster, including Margaret Fell, wife of Judge Fell, who was to become Fox's wife following the death of the judge.

THE GOSSIPS' BRIDLE (THE BRANK) 1927 80517

Whilst the bridle was used to punish gossips, it was also used on Quaker women to stop them preaching, in at least Carlisle if not Lancaster itself. The bridle was very heavy to wear. A bar went into the victim's mouth to hold down her tongue and prevent her from speaking.

William Stout was a Quaker and also a Lancaster trader. He lived from 1665 to 1752, and wrote an autobiography, from which comes much of the information we have about trading at the time. He was an ironmonger and a grocer, and his premises appear to have been around the corner of Market Street and Cheapside. He started up on his own in 1688, having served an apprenticeship under Henry Coward. Before finishing his apprenticeship, Stout went to London to purchase goods for his own shop; these were sent back to Lancaster by sea. His main trading was done on the Saturday market days. Stout's stocks included iron goods, tobacco, sugar and prunes.

Stout tells that in 1688 he boarded with Alderman Thomas Baynes at a rent of five

CHURCH STREET 1896 37381

We are looking westwards up Church Street towards the priory church. The buildings on the right are not much changed today.

pounds a year. However, he often lodged in his shop, as he was frequently called up 'at all times of the night to serve customers'. His sister, Elin, often came to assist on market days.

Bartering was common at that time, but Stout strongly disapproved of it, believing that a fair price should be fixed for goods. When not about his business duties, Stout studied religious and other books, and in the evenings he walked on Green Ayre. He tells how in 1691 and 1692 his next door neighbour, a good customer to the ironmongery business, was a part-owner of freight ships to Virginia; this neighbour sold tobacco consigned to him on to Stout, who then imported it and paid the duty.

Stout writes of a major fire in Lancaster in 1698 when over twenty dwellings were burned down. It started when a certain Ann Tinkler

PENNY'S HOSPITAL

Charitable work is a Lancaster tradition. In 1720 the Penny Almshouses were completed; the money for them had been left by William Penny, a former mayor, in 1716. The buildings, in a courtyard off King Street (then Back Lane), were thatched at that time. They were established for twelve poor, indigent men of the town unless there was a shortage of men, when women then qualified.

PENNY'S HOSPITAL, ALMSHOUSES IN KING STREET 2004 L10702k (Robert Swain)

took out ashes that had not been properly quenched, and a spark must have flown up to the thatched roof under six feet from where she left them. The east wind caused the fire to spread quickly, so that people did not have time to rescue their possessions, and it burned much of the north side of the street (probably Church Street); but two buildings were saved, as they were built of stone and roofed with slate. The loss of property came to over £2,000. From then, stone rather than timber and thatch was used for building.

In 1697 Stout stopped trading in Lancaster for a while; he transferred his business to his apprentice, and went in for the shipping trade. Before setting out on that venture he totalled up his books, and found that in the nine years he had traded he had lost £220 to 248 insolvent debtors. His own wealth by then amounted to £1,100, and this, he proudly says, was without 'prosecuting any debter'. The shipping trade was not a success for Stout, and in 1704 he returned to trading in Lancaster. He took back his old business, for John Troughton, Stout's former apprentice, was in prison for debt. Stout paid the full market price for the stock so that Troughton's creditors received as much as possible.

In 1724 there was an accident in Stout's shop when his nephew, also called William, was serving a lad who came in for a pipe of tobacco. Unbeknown to the lad, William put a little gunpowder into it, but he did not shut the drawer properly from which he had taken it. The lad started to smoke the pipe and the powder in it fired, sending a spark into the powder drawer. There were three to four pounds of powder in the drawer, which blew up. Fortunately the doors and windows were open, or the blast would have blown up the shop. The lad and William and Stout's maid were burned but not killed, to the surprise of those outside the shop who saw and heard the blast, and saw how boxes and goods were scattered around.

John Hodgson was an Alderman and four times Mayor of Lancaster; he was well known to William Stout. By trade he was a grocer and apothecary. He had great success with the Virginia trade, having jointly purchased with his brother-in-law a ship captured from the Dutch. This vessel was the first from Lancaster to sail to Virginia, and the start in the early 1680s of what was to become very important trade for the town. Hodgson also imported goods from Bordeaux in France, such as wine, brandy and prunes. He had a sugar house in Lancaster for refining raw sugar, which was brought up from Bristol. This building may have later been sold to Robert Lawson; it is now remembered in the name Sugar House Alley.

With his wealth, Hodgson built himself a house costing £1,000, a considerable sum for the times. He took some gentlemen's sons on as apprentices, and they, together with the servants, 'made too free with his wine sellers (cellars) and ware houses'. The lavish lifestyle was something Hodgson enjoyed, and he entertained wealthy country gentlemen from around the district; his household expenses were £500 a year. However, he got into financial difficulties, and owed Customs dues of over £2,280 in 1701, the last year in which he was mayor. As a result he went bankrupt, and ended up in prison in Lancaster Castle, where he died.

The castle had become a debtors' prison as well as housing criminals by the 18th century – at that time it was very easy to fall into debt. Some people, who had wealthy friends, and having arranged their own arrest, went into prison voluntarily and rented rooms there - the charge was between 5s and £1 15s, depending on their comfort. Once in prison they could not be forced to pay their debts. Friends and relatives could visit from 8.00 am to 8.00 pm. One Lancaster lady left money to pay for a prisoner's accommodation and also to pay the fees of a clergyman to preach to the inmates. Several Lancaster merchants ended up going bankrupt over the years.

In 1743, so as to make the sound travel further, a new peal of bells was purchased for St Mary's, the parish church. The churchwardens decided that the tower should be extended 'ten yards higher'; this put a considerable strain on it, and it started to collapse. It was necessary, therefore, to have the old tower demolished and a new one built - the architect was Henry Sephton from Liverpool. This is the tower we see today (80521, page 33), and explains why the design is different from the rest of the church, which dates from the late 15th century.

REVERSE OF A DEBTOR'S HALFPENNY 2004
ZZZ00479 (Courtesy of Eric Wilkinson)

OBVERSE OF A DEBTOR'S HALFPENNY 2004
ZZZ00480 (Courtesy of Eric Wilkinson)

A 'Debtor's Halfpenny' was a coin only redeemable in Lancaster and Bristol Gaols. John Howard, the prison reformer, is shown on the obverse.

THE PARISH CHURCH 1927 80521

SANCTUARY

The privilege of sanctuary existed at St Mary's Church from when it was first built until the right to claim sanctuary was finally extinguished during the reign of Charles I. At Battle Abbey, the Charter said: 'If any thief or murderer or person guilty of any other crime, fly for fear of death, and come to this church, let him have no harm, but be freely dismissed'. A similar right would apply to Lancaster. After the Reformation, the privilege no longer applied for murder and other such serious crimes. The right of sanctuary in Lancashire was then confined to Lancaster and Manchester, and later to Lancaster alone. A special building housing asylum seekers is believed to have stood near the church.

The overseas and coastal trades required ships, and several vessels were built locally. The Brockbank family were the main shipbuilders in the town; first, from the 1730s, came George Brockbank, followed by his son and his son's nephew. Their yard was where a part of Sainsbury's now stands. The Brockbank yard built ships of all sizes. The average was just under 200 tons, but five were over 300 tons. Besides going to local owners, their vessels went to London, Greenock and even to the West Indies.

One problem that the Brockbanks had was the old medieval four-arched bridge spanning the Lune, roughly where the Millennium Bridge now stands. It was constructed of stone, and was the only bridge across the river between the sea and Loyne Bridge, which spans the river between Hornby and Gressingham. During the 1745 Jacobite Rising, parts of its battlements had been removed to reveal any forces crossing it. Colonel Charteris of the English forces would have demolished the bridge to deny its use to the Scottish forces, but local people pointed out that the river was still fordable at low tide. The arches of

the bridge meant that ships had to be de-masted before they could pass under it when leaving the yard, but more of this later (at the end of Chapter Two).

Robert Gillow came to Lancaster from Singleton in the Fylde to serve his apprenticeship as a joiner under John Robinson, something which would have cost his widowed mother around £40. This was probably around 1721, as he became a Freeman in 1727/28. The Gillow family were Roman Catholics at a time when this was generally a disadvantage, but it may well have helped Robert, as this was his master's denomination. Following his apprenticeship, he was able to be presented to the town Bailiffs and pay the fine (a fee) to practise his trade in the town.

The firm that he founded was known as Gillow's, and it was generally known by that name over the following years regardless of its official title at the time. Robert imported timber from Jamaica, Cuba and Honduras, in particular mahogany; he also imported rum and sugar. The timber was made into fine furniture, which was sold to the slave-owning families in the West Indies. His business did many carpentry jobs, even just putting up a shelf, and made coffins, mangles, troughs for hens, and other such goods.

Gillow's prospered, and Robert's two sons, Richard and Robert, joined him in the business. Lancaster's position on the west coast and its trade with the West Indies made it ideal for the mahogany trade to develop. However, Gillow's also dealt in other goods, exporting flour, cotton goods, shoes and

certain. Numbers 1 and 3 Cable Street is one building (64221, below right-hand-side), and the Custom House is the other.

Lancaster became wealthy in Georgian times, resulting in the erection of fine Georgian buildings, many of which still stand today. Local stone was readily available, in particular where polished freestone was needed – this was sandstone rubbed to a flat finish. Mainly, this stone came from Lancaster Moor (where there were a number of quarries in the 18th

CABLE STREET 1912 64221

potatoes, which were packed into the larger pieces of furniture to enable more economical loads to be carried on the ships.

Besides being a furniture maker, Richard Gillow was an architect. It is not known exactly how many of Lancaster's buildings he was responsible for, but two are known for

century), Scotforth and Ellel. This stone is used for the pillars of the Custom House (each pillar is carved from a single piece of stone); it is described as 'beautifully veined', which is caused by iron impurities within the stone causing brownish streaks.

CHURCH STREET 1886 18092

Among the many Georgian buildings of Lancaster is Number 76 Church Street, the town house of the Marton family (left). It was re-fronted in the 1730s or 40s. Inside is some fine oak panelling, and outside is a conical hood, which is a link snuffer for snuffing out the flames of torches. It is often said that Bonnie Prince Charlie stayed here during the 1745 Rising, but it is probable that he only dined in the house, staying the night at another Church Street building. Further down is the former Masonic Hall at the corner of New Road, now demolished and replaced by a modern building.

ST MARY'S GATE c1955 L10041

ST MARY'S GATE 2004 L10703k (Robert Swain)

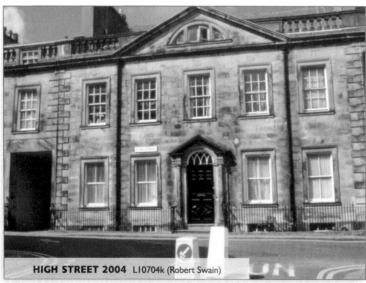

HIGH STREET 2004 L10704k (Robert Swain)

This house in High Street, at the top of Middle Street, was built for a Lancaster solicitor in around 1770, and is one of the finest in the town.

St Mary's Gate, below the priory church ('gate' here is derived from the Old Norse word 'gata', meaning a road, and not a gate in a town wall) still has good examples of Georgian architecture (see above); the slope provided carriage entrances beneath some of the buildings.

High Street and Queen Street have a number of Georgian buildings. The Trinity United Reformed Church dates from 1773, when it was built as an independent chapel.

THE DISPENSARY

The monks provided the first healthcare in Lancaster. It was not until 1781 that concern was raised about providing care for the people of the town. At that time Dr David Campbell organised a meeting, and it was decided to provide a dispensary for 'furnishing the sick poor with medical advice and medicine gratis'. This first dispensary was at Dr Campbell's own house, which was demolished when the Storey Institute was extended. A new building was acquired on Castle Hill in 1785, and it was in use until 1833 (L10007, below).

CASTLE HILL c1950 L10007

The right-hand building was the second dispensary. Next to it is what is now the Cottage Museum; the middle door then was a passageway.

Lancaster was one of the first towns in the country to get a dispensary. Above the doorway of each of the buildings that housed a dispensary was a rectangular space for a plaque. The plaque illustrated the parable of the Good Samaritan, which was appropriate for these buildings dispensing medical care. It is still to be seen today above the original entrance to the Royal Lancaster Infirmary.

THE COTTAGE MUSEUM, CASTLE HILL 2004 L10705k
(Robert Swain)

The Grand Theatre is the third oldest provincial theatre in Britain - it dates from 1782. Its building was largely financed by public subscription. There were plans to demolish the theatre after its closure in 1950 (at that time it was a cinema). The Lancaster Footlights Club raised £7,000 to purchase the building and have done much excellent work to it since then, and many productions are put on there during the course of a year.

Lancaster was under the head-port of Chester until 1732, and its officers were appointed as deputies of those in Chester.

The original Custom House was above the old bridge, and in 1732 a new Custom House was built below the bridge. By the 1740s, the town was desperately in need of a proper quay for its shipping to load and unload, and in 1749 the Lancaster Port Commissioners were established by an Act of Parliament. A year later the construction of St George's Quay was begun - a wall was built at the low tide line and the space behind was filled in. Houses, shops and warehouses were built; the older warehouses were of three storeys, rising to five storeys for the newer ones.

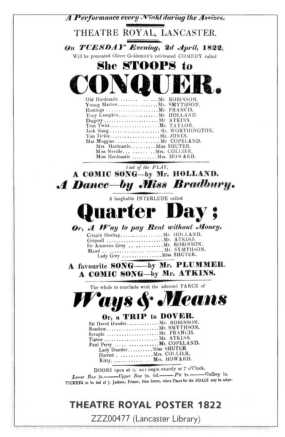

THEATRE ROYAL POSTER 1822

ZZZ00477 (Lancaster Library)

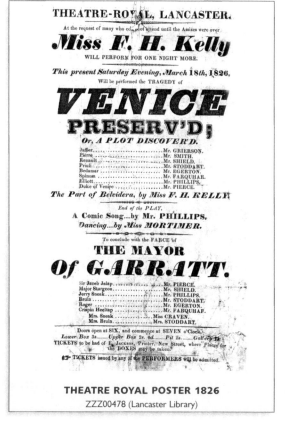

THEATRE ROYAL POSTER 1826

ZZZ00478 (Lancaster Library)

The Theatre Royal is a former name of the Grand Theatre.
Note how entertainment had been put on for the time of the Assizes.

LANCASTER FOOTLIGHTS PROGRAMME ZZZ00450
(Lancaster Footlights Club)

LANCASTER FOOTLIGHTS PROGRAMME ZZZ00451
(Lancaster Footlights Club)

A space was left between the warehouses, presumably in anticipation of a new Custom House. This was built in 1762 to Richard Gillow's design. At ground level was the Weigh House, where goods were weighed before being placed in bonded warehouses. Boatmen and others would wait here when on call. The first floor could not be reached from indoors, but only by using the outside steps. These led straight into the Long Room, where the clerks sat and where the business with the ships' masters and the merchants were transacted. Beside it was the Collector's office for collecting the dues, together with other offices.

The old bridge over the Lune was reached down Bridge Lane, which began by Covell Cross at the top of Church Street, and passed by the Three Mariners – at this point there is the only remaining part of the original road

to St George's Quay. Particularly since 1745, when the parapets had been demolished, the bridge had become unsafe, and there were a number of accidents. On one occasion a woman was leading a horse and cart full of coal across the bridge when the linchpin on one of the wheels broke and they all fell over the side of the bridge. The horse was killed, the cart smashed and the woman 'a good deal hurt'. A new bridge giving better access to the town needed to be built, and on a route that was less congested than having to cross over the Quay to reach it. The architect Thomas Harrison had designed bridges in Rome, and he won the competition for the new Skerton Bridge (L10706k, page 44). He designed a bridge with five arches, but with a level roadway, the first in this country - previous bridges had been bowed at the centre. Another special feature is the five

SKERTON BRIDGE 2004 L10706k (Robert Swain)

relieving arches to increase the water flow at times of heavy flooding. Harrison's bridge cost £14,000, and was opened in October 1788.

Another of Harrison's works was the rebuilding of Lancaster Castle; he was commissioned as architect for the work in 1788. It is mostly his work that we see today. He altered Hadrian's Tower, removing the ceilings and raising it to its present height. His Grand Jury Room is perfectly round, and it is believed that Harrison insisted that the two doors be constructed with a curve to conform to this. His work also included the magnificent Shire Hall, the Crown Court and the barristers' rooms. He was responsible for part of the prison, and most of the exterior walling – he made the castle larger than it was in medieval times. The Grand Jury Room and the courts were largely furnished by Gillow's, and are a tribute to their craftsmen.

Gillow's continued to prosper following the death of Robert (senior) in 1772. Richard continued to run the Lancaster end of the business, whilst his brother Robert ran the London branch that they had opened. In the second half of the 18th century and into the early 19th century they made some of the finest English furniture, examples of which are to be seen in the Judges' Lodgings. The telescopic table was Richard's invention; a sketch in the cost book for 1795 shows an example twenty-four feet in length and of ten sections.

THE CASTLE FROM ST MARY'S CHURCH 1886 18084

THE CASTLE, THE SHIRE HALL 1896 37370

The cannon outside the Shire Hall were relics of the Crimean War. They were lost in the scrap metal drive of the Second World War.

Fact File

Above the gateway into Lancaster Castle is a statue of John o'Gaunt carved by Claude Nimmo, but it was modelled by a Gillow's cabinetmaker named Beckett. When he was a very old man, Beckett was passing by when he saw a stranger admiring the statue. The stranger said to him, 'The head of the man who made that does not ache now'. Beckett replied, 'Well, it was aching yesterday', and went on to tell of how he had made the model many years earlier.

A reminder of that period in the firm's history is the building at the bottom of Castle Hill, which still bears the name Gillow's above its doorway.

For a time in the 18th century the Roman Catholics in Lancaster used a building in St Leonardgate for worship. However, in 1798 a new building was erected on the northern side of Dalton Square; Richard Gillow was one of the principal contributors towards its cost. After the new building came into use, the old church was sold to Gillow's, who used it as a store. Later, after the present St Peter's Cathedral was completed in 1859, the Dalton Square church was to become the County Cinema. It was to later lie derelict for many years before being taken over by Lancaster City Council to house the planning department. Elements of the former church were retained when the architect drew up the plans for Palatine Hall.

Other towns had become linked to each other by canal by now, but Lancaster was out on a limb. A canal between Kendal, Lancaster, Preston and beyond had been discussed several times over the years, and surveys had been made. By 1791 patience was running out, and on 4 June thirty Lancaster merchants and traders petitioned the mayor to convene a public meeting to consider the making of a canal linking Lancaster to the Leeds and Liverpool Canal. Only four days later, on 8 June, it was resolved to promote a canal, and a subscription list was started.

The Canal Committee was not satisfied with the earlier lines surveyed, and in October 1791 they appointed John Rennie to survey a route. A broad canal was needed to carry larger and longer boats than those on some other canals. This would enable coal to be carried from south Lancashire through to Kendal, and large quantities of limestone in the opposite direction. John Rennie's survey included a deep cutting to the south of Lancaster, and a lower crossing of the Lune than in the earlier surveys. The next stage was another meeting in the town hall on 7 February 1792, when it was unanimously resolved that an Act of Parliament be obtained to build the Lancaster Canal, running from West Houghton in the south of the county through to Kendal.

The first chairman of the Lancaster Canal Company was John Dilworth, one of Lancaster's two bankers, and one of the petitioners for it to be built. The other banker, Thomas Worswick, was elected treasurer. Amongst the other petitioners were John Brockbank the shipbuilder, the Earl of Balcarres, who was a coal mine owner, and John Wakefield of Kendal, owner of a gunpowder works. The canal committee was formed from Lancaster men, apart from one each from Kendal and Preston.

The construction of the canal started in 1793, and went ahead not without its problems. It was not until January 1794 that works started on John Rennie's Lune aqueduct (28608, page 47). The original specifications of the aqueduct are signed by John Rennie and by Alexander Stevens from Edinburgh. Stevens and his son were architects from Edinburgh, and responsible for the building of the bridge.

THE RIVER LUNE 1918 68331

Lune Bank Gardens, from where this picture was taken, were a gift of Lord Ashton. The aqueduct is in the distance.

JOHN RENNIE'S LUNE AQUEDUCT

John Rennie's Lune aqueduct is 600 feet long. Piles about 20 feet long were driven into the bed of the river to make a foundation for the piers, which go down to 20 feet below Skerton Weir. The piers alone cost just over £14,790. Rennie wanted to build the aqueduct of brick, but the committee would have none of that, for Lancaster was built in stone. This greatly increased the costs, so that there was too little money to cross the River Ribble; this resulted in there being no link by water between the Ribble and the main canal system until the opening of the Millennium Ribble Link in July 2002. The original estimate for building the aqueduct was £18,618 16s, but the final total was £48,320 18s 10d.

THE AQUEDUCT 1891 28608

The Lancaster Canal was formerly opened between Preston and Tewitfield on 22 November 1797. A cavalcade of six boats took part in the opening ceremony, but the journey was only from Fryerage Bridge to the aqueduct and back. The Committee were to meet at the company's offices by Aldcliffe Road at 9.30 am and proceed to the Fryerage 'accompanied with colours and music'. Afterwards, there was a procession to

DEEP CUTTING AND BROKEN BACK BRIDGE

At the southern end of Lancaster, so as to avoid going a long way round, the canal had to be cut through Burrow Heights, thus forming Deep Cutting, which is about a mile and a half long. The deepest part is by the Cockerham Road Bridge, which is much widened from its original state. In places the canal is not lined, but cut straight through the bedrock. Along this stretch is the unusual bridge which is officially Carr Lane Bridge, but generally known as Broken Back Bridge. It is thought that it got this name because the roadway on either side drops down to the centre of the bridge rather than its being hump-backed like the other standard bridges. During the cutting of the canal, some navvies dug up sculptures from Roman times.

BROKEN BACK BRIDGE 1891 28612

the King's Arms Hotel to dine. Volleys were fired at various points, the final one being in front of the Town Hall in Market Square.

A year earlier there had been problems with the market, as hucksters and higglers (both words had very similar meanings, and here would refer to pedlars and similar people given to bartering merchandise) were buying up fruit, eggs, butter and other provisions only to sell them again to the townspeople for a higher price. This led to an order that if they bought any produce before 11 am they would be prosecuted.

By that time, Market Square had been encroached upon by buildings, in particular by the third Town Hall, now the City Museum, which was completed in 1783 (1809 1p, page 50-51). Then, the ground floor was an open area housing the grain and butter markets. There were gates between the arches, which were closed when the Mayor came on his monthly visit to 'assay and weigh butter and bread' in his capacity as the Clerk of Markets.

On 5 September 1800, John Brockbank purchased the materials of the old bridge (following the opening of Skerton Bridge it was no longer in use) from two Lancaster JPs, Edmund Rigby and John Bradshaw. He agreed to pay off £250 for the rights and interests in the bridge to Richard Mason of Bridge Lane for possible damage to him. Brockbank removed the first of the arches in 1802 to allow ships to pass down the river without their masts having to be removed. A second arch fell down in 1807,

another was demolished in 1814, and the final one fell in 1845. Following on from this, Brockbank paid £30 to the Lancaster Port Commissioners for them to take from him all 'the Rights and Interest of the said John Brockbank' in the ruins and site of the Old Bridge.

Following the opening of the canal, Lancaster developed a textile industry. The mills were sited along the canal banks and not in the town itself. The first mill to be built was White Cross Mills in 1802 for Thomas Mason and Co, and it was the first mill in the town to make full use of steam power before the 1820s. Other mills followed, such as Moor Lane (north), Moor Lane (south) and Albion Mill.

The period of the fifty years up to 1800 can be said to be the peak of Lancaster's prosperity. From then on, big changes took place. The West Indies trade declined, partly because of the emergence of Liverpool as a major port. As for slave trading, as far as is known no slaves were landed at Lancaster; the slaves were taken directly from Africa to the West Indies. The trade was later transferred to Liverpool, and then abolished in 1807. The trade was not looked upon as a disgrace before that time, and at least two masters of slave ships went on to become mayors of Lancaster. Various traders and merchants either moved from town or ceased trading. This stagnation resulted in the Georgian buildings in the town being retained, and not swept away in Victorian times.

THE TOWN HALL 1886 18091p

CHAPTER THREE

CHANGES AND THE VICTORIAN ERA

TRADE in Lancaster decreased in the early 1800s, partly owing to the wars with France, partly to the growth of the port of Liverpool, and partly owing to other factors. Baines records in 1824 how 25,000 pieces of sailcloth a year were manufactured in the five years to 1800, but by the time he was writing, production had dropped to less than twenty a week. There were then three cotton mills working in Lancaster, and a mill spinning fine worsted yarn.

In 1822 Worswick's bank failed, and four years later Dilworth & Company went the same way – both these banks had been privately owned. Many people in the town lost money with these two failures, and Lancaster was left with no bank; the nearest was in Kirkby Lonsdale. Largely through the influence of Gillow's, it was resolved at a public meeting that a joint-stock bank be

★ COURTESY

　★ FRIENDLINESS

　　★ EFFICIENCY

The dictionary tells us that service is work done in response to some general need. But that is a definition of the bare bones, the anatomy of service. It includes service which, although perhaps efficient, has descended into chilly politeness.

That, however, is not the District Bank's way. If you appreciate willingness and enthusiasm, if you are looking for efficient service rendered with courtesy and friendship — then bank with . . .

DISTRICT BANK
LIMITED

THE OLDEST JOINT STOCK BANK IN ENGLAND

Local Offices at :—
CHURCH ST. and PENNY ST., LANCASTER
and at CATON, HEST BANK and HORNBY

DISTRICT BANK ADVERTISEMENT ZZZ00453
(Reproduced by kind permission of Lancaster City Council)

Fact File

Sir Richard Owen was born in a now demolished house on the corner of Brock Street and Thurnham Street in 1804. He attended Lancaster Grammar School, then close by the castle, leaving there in 1819. He undertook medical training, which gave him the opportunity to study anatomy, and became a member of the Royal College of Surgeons in 1826. His interest in anatomy was of great use when studying fossil remains of extinct creatures. He named these 'dinosaurs', the word we still use today.

established. As a result, the Lancaster Banking Company was set up. The bank was the first joint-stock bank in the country; it was later converted to a limited liability company, with Leonard Redmayne, a partner in Gillow's, as its first chairman. The National Westminster Bank in Church Street is a direct descendant of that bank.

Changes happened at the castle. Whilst the area to the north of the Shire Hall and below the priory is now used as a car park, it used to be the place where prisoners met their doom – it was called Hanging Corner. From 1800 criminals were publicly hanged here instead of being taken to the Moor. People came from all over the district around Lancaster and from Preston and the Fylde to witness hangings, which usually took place on a Saturday. The Rev Joseph Rowley was prison chaplain for fifty-four years from 1804. He saw more public hangings than anybody else in Lancaster, attending 168. He was also master of the nearby Free School for twenty-three years, during which time he considered boys would gain a respect for the law by watching hangings and gave them a half day holiday to go to watch. Hanging days were good for the shops, which did a great trade - people would arrive in the town from daybreak.

In 1832, capital punishment was abolished for various crimes such as forgery, the theft of goods or animals, and highway robbery, so the number of hangings at the castle fell. Instead, people were often transported to the colonies, such as Australia. Public executions were abolished from 1868; the last one in Lancaster was in 1865. Thomas Rawcliffe, who used to live in a house behind Cheapside, was the last man to be executed in Lancaster Castle on 15 November 1910 – he had strangled his wife.

THE CASTLE, THE EXECUTION CHAIR 1927 80519

Jane Scott, a crippled teenage girl, was found guilty of murdering her mother in Preston, and was sentenced to death in March 1828. After she had been sentenced to death, she also confessed to murdering her father, a child of her own, and her sister's boy. In prison she had become so weak from self-imposed starvation that a special wooden chair had to be made to wheel her out to the gallows.

THE BRANDING IRON

The branding iron is still to be seen in the Assize Court, and was used up to the early 19th century when a prisoner had been found guilty of a crime. The red-hot iron applied the letter 'M' to the prisoner's hand, which was held tightly by two iron hoops. If a clear mark had been made, the brander would turn to the judge and say, 'A fair mark, my lord'. The letter 'M' stood for malefactor, or evildoer. The mark was permanent, and thus betrayed the fact that the prisoner had been before the courts.

THE CASTLE, THE BRANDING IRON 1936 87342

In 1819 the Lancaster Canal was opened right through to Kendal. It was not until 1826 that the Glasson Arm was completed, linking the canal with the sea. The canal helped Lancaster to survive the loss of the sea trade. However, trade continued to decline, so in 1882 the Customs were moved to Barrow and the Custom House was from then used for other purposes.

At a meeting in the Town Hall in 1836, the idea of a railway line to Lancaster was put forward. This was the Lancaster & Preston Junction Railway, which opened on 25 June 1840; its station is still standing and in use as a nurses' home opposite the Infirmary.

Later, the Lancaster and Carlisle line followed, and then the line from Yorkshire through Green Ayre station, across Greyhound Bridge and onto Morecambe, with a branch to Lancaster Castle station. Also, a branch line from Castle station was built to Glasson Dock.

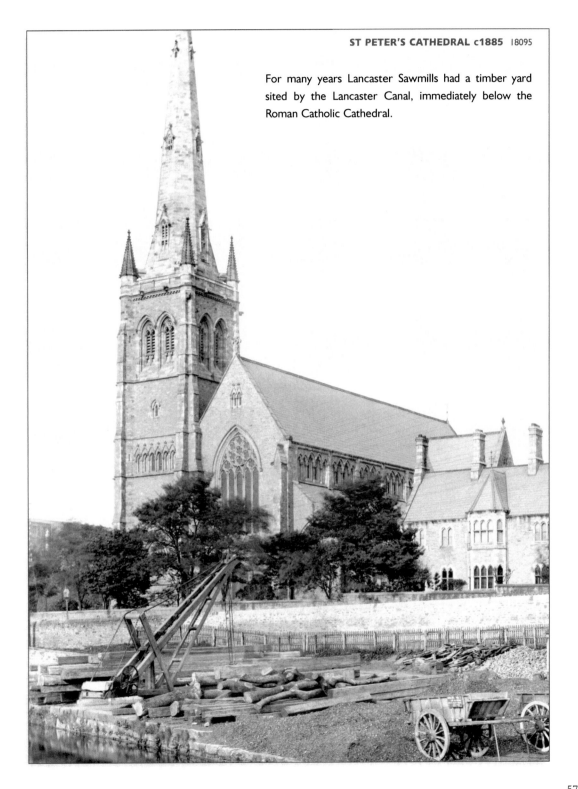

ST PETER'S CATHEDRAL c1885 18095

For many years Lancaster Sawmills had a timber yard sited by the Lancaster Canal, immediately below the Roman Catholic Cathedral.

THE RAILWAY BRIDGES

Motorists crossing Greyhound Bridge today are using the third bridge to take the railway line from Green Ayre station across to the Skerton bank of the Lune. The first bridge was opened in 1846 for the North Western railway line from Yorkshire to Morecambe, and was built on piles of timber. It was replaced in 1864 by the iron bridge seen in this photograph. In 1911, a similar bridge, the present one, was built, but about 30 feet downstream. In 1908 the railway line from Castle Station, via Green Ayre and on to Morecambe and Heysham, was electrified. The last electric train ran across it on 1 January 1966. Green Ayre station, to the left, has been demolished. Fairclough's modified the bridge in 1971 by laying a broader concrete deck on top of the girders, giving a 30-foot roadway plus a pathway and verge.

FROM SKERTON BRIDGE 1891 28599a

However, big changes were about to happen, thanks to the businessmen James Williamson and the Storey brothers. James Williamson (Senior) came to Lancaster from Keswick in 1827 and was apprenticed to Richard Hutton, a master painter. After his apprenticeship he went to London, where he saw table baize (or oilcloth) being manufactured by a slow and labour-intensive process. He experimented on this over the years, including the time after his return to Lancaster, where he at first set up as a painter and decorator. 1844 saw him set up in business producing oilcloth. As his business expanded, he established a small factory just above Carlisle Bridge, and in 1854 he bought some land below the bridge, where St George's Works was built.

Bath Mill was bought in 1864, and in the same year Greenfield Mill was built; both mills were to produce the cotton cloth as backing for the oilcloth produced on the Quay. In 1870 Williamson bought the land owned by the then defunct Lancaster Shipbuilding Company, an ill-fated attempt to bring back shipbuilding to the town. Once the new mills were built, the workforce expanded considerably from 70 in 1852 to over 2,000 in 1879.

THE VIEW FROM THE CASTLE 1927 80505

This view looks across Giant Axe Field to the chimneys of the Williamson factory at Lune Mills beyond.

LOCAL INDUSTRIES AND THE RAILWAYS

Scale Ford was an ancient crossing place on the River Lune – it was fordable at low tide. Part of Lancaster's gasworks is on the left. There were railway sidings branching from the Glasson Dock line from Lancaster Castle station; these ran up New Quay to Carlisle Bridge to serve Williamson's and to bring coal to the gasworks. The tracks crossed St George's Quay by the main entrance to Williamson's, but they have long since been removed. Williamson's also had their own narrow gauge railway line which took the ash from the boiler house to a tip by Freeman's Woods and carried goods from the Quay. Lune Mills is to the right of the picture.

FROM SCALE FORD 1918 68329

ESTD. 1844

WILLIAMSON LINOLEUM
LANCASTREUM FELT BASE
DADOLIN WALLCOVERING

LANCASTER CLOTH
LIONETTE SQUARES
LIONIDE LEATHERCLOTH

Jas. Williamson & Son Ltd.
LANCASTER
Telephone 5222

BRANCHES: LONDON. MANCHESTER. BIRMINGHAM GLASGOW
AGENTS THROUGHOUT THE WORLD

LUNE MILLS, LANCASTER

WILLIAMSON'S ADVERTISEMENT c1955 ZZZ00456

(Reproduced by kind permission of Lancaster City Council)

Fact File

At Golgotha, close to the southern gates of Williamson Park, stands a row of cottages dating back to the 17th century. The 1881 census shows that most of them, 20 out of 22, were occupied by laundresses. Probably they used this area as it was high above the soot and grime of the town centre, and well exposed to winds with which to dry the laundry. Also, it would be safe from theft, something which regularly used to occur in the town.

Williamson set up a Ragged School in Aldcliffe Lane and financed the laying out of Williamson Park on the site of former quarries (18097, page 61). Work had started during the American War of Independence when the supply of raw cotton was interrupted, causing Lancaster's industry to suffer. Then an unknown benefactor had a carriage drive and gravel paths constructed. However, it was James Williamson who converted the moorland into a park, something which took place between 1879 and 1881 and cost about £13,250. He did not see the fruition of the project, as he died in 1879. In 1881 the park was handed over to Lancaster Corporation by his son, but work continued on it long after that.

Meanwhile, in the autumn of 1835 William and Thomas Storey had come with their parents, brothers and sisters across Morecambe Bay from Bardsea, near Ulverston, to live on Damside Street. William, who was twelve years old, soon sought an apprenticeship in painting and decorating; he was taken on by Richard Hutton, where he met another apprentice, older than himself, James Williamson. It is remarkable that these two people who were to have so much influence over Lancaster were both apprentices to the same man. Whether or not William Storey knew of Williamson's experiments on oilcloth is not known. However, after Williamson's return from London, the opportunity came for Storey to work for him and gain experience in that way. A few years later he was in business with two partners as 'Painters, Japanners and

WILLIAMSON PARK c1885 18097

Table Cover Manufacturers'. By April 1851 that partnership had been totally dissolved, and in the same year his brother Thomas joined William in the business at their workshop at 47 St George's Quay. The business was a success, and, at different times, both brothers were mayors of Lancaster. In 1856, the brothers took over White Cross Mill (see pages 65 and 66) at the top of Penny Street from Satterthwaite and Barrow, and soon afterwards Moor Lane Mill, where Thomas had worked as a child. By 1864 most of Lancaster's cotton mills were owned by Storey Brothers or Williamson.

William Storey became a director of the unsuccessful shipbuilding company that was formed in 1863 - Williamson bought the land on its failure. For a time William Storey was also the secretary of the Mechanics' Institute, which was to become the Storey Institute.

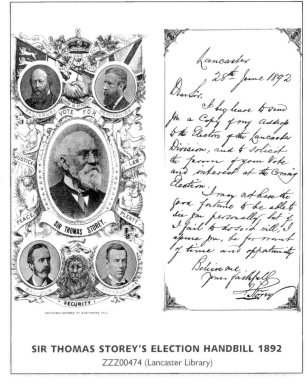

SIR THOMAS STOREY'S ELECTION HANDBILL 1892
ZZZ00474 (Lancaster Library)

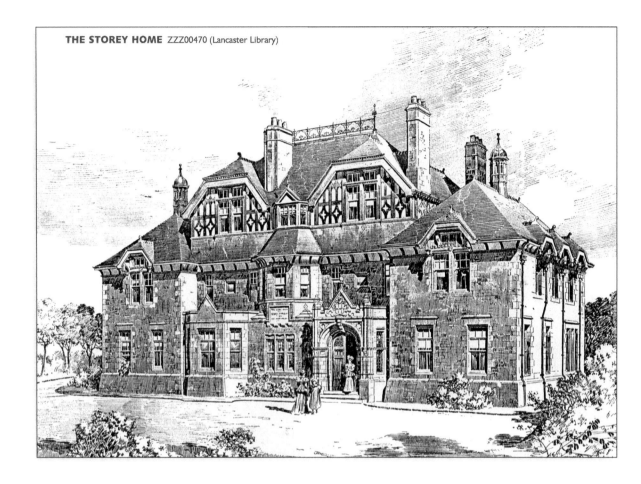

THE STOREY HOME ZZZ00470 (Lancaster Library)

Thomas Storey, too, started work when he was about twelve years old, working in Moor Lane Mill; by the age of fourteen he was keeping the books and making up the wages. Illness led him for a while to work as a surveyor for his elder brother John and later for another surveyor, Edmund Sharpe, before Storey Brothers was founded. He gave generously of his time and money to both the Royal Albert Asylum and the Royal Lancaster Infirmary. In 1887 the Trustees of the Mechanics' Institute asked him to accept the existing institute so that he could carry out his plans for it. The Storey Institute and

Technical College (28605) was opened in 1891 as an art gallery and institute for technical education. The building cost £12,000, but Storey also gave pictures and busts, adding considerably to his costs. He died in December 1898, having been looked on as a kind and humane employer.

Another brother was Edward Storey, who was trained as an engineer at the Mechanics' Institute. He went to work at the Phoenix Foundry, where Thomas was first a partner and then owner. Although there is no record of it, Edward's skills as an engineer must have been used by Storey Brothers.

THE STOREY INSTITUTE 1891 28605

TWO PUBLIC HOUSES

On the left is the White Cross Hotel, now the Farmers Arms. The name White Cross probably comes from a prayer cross that stood here at the edge of the town many centuries ago; here travellers would offer prayers of thankfulness for their safe arrival. Opposite, the Alexandra Hotel and the adjacent buildings occupy the site of an inn, the Prince William Henry, and its surrounding fields, which were used as a fairground and football field and for other similar activities. In the pub in the 1890s, many pints of beer were drawn by 5.50 am ready for the Storey Brothers' workers to drink before starting work at 6.00 am.

PENNY STREET c1955 L10026

Fact File

From 1855 to 1881 the Royal Lancashire Militia occupied Springfield Barracks, a then new building at White Cross. The militia, a reserve force, had adequate accommodation for all personnel: officers had the left of the main building, and the sergeants' quarters were on the right. In front was the parade ground, whilst flanking South Road were the guardroom and cells. The militia became part of the King's Own and moved to Bowerham Barracks in 1881.

The frontage at White Cross, which in the 19th Century was the depot of the Yeomanry and Artillery, and is now the Social Club of the Company.

STOREYS OF LANCASTER ADVERTISEMENT ZZZ00454 (Reproduced by kind permission of Lancaster City Council)

WHITE CROSS MILL 2004 L10709k (Robert Swain)

To the left of the former barracks is the gatehouse and entrance to the mill complex.

James Williamson Junior was born on 31 December 1842 and educated at Lancaster Royal Grammar School. On leaving school he entered his father's oilcloth business, and took full control of it in about 1875 owing to his father's ill health. It was he who introduced the production of linoleum and also window blind cloth, 'a New Material entirely superseding the Old Fashioned Blinds', according to an advertisement of the time. This was to lead to the prosperity of the firm and its major expansion alongside the River Lune.

He was very concerned with local affairs: he was a town councillor from 1871 to 1880, High Sheriff of Lancaster in 1885, and

Liberal MP for the town between 1886 and 1895. He was then elevated to the Lords as Baron Ashton of Ashton – he chose the title from his Ashton Hall estate to the south of the town, which he had bought in 1884. The estate had its own private railway platform on the line from Lancaster to Glasson Dock.

Lord Ashton's main home in Lancaster, where he died in 1930, was Ryelands House across the Lune in Skerton (L10002, page 67), an area where many of his employees lived. It was built in 1836 for Jonathan Dunn, who was twice Mayor of Lancaster, and was extended after Lord Ashton purchased it in 1883. Then he had an extension built at the back of the house, which included the

RYELANDS HOUSE c1955 L10002

tower; it was designed by Paley & Austin, the well-known Lancaster architects (see L10003, below). Also, to protect his privacy, a high perimeter wall surrounded the property, which has now been brought down to ground level. It is often said that Lord Ashton had a telescope set up in Ryelands House so that he could look across the Lune to St George's Quay to see which of his employees were arriving late for work.

RYELANDS PARK c1955 L10003

One other large employer of the second half of the 19th century is often overlooked. The Lancaster Wagon Company Limited was started alongside Caton Road in 1863, and some of its buildings still stand (L10710k, page 69). The company's works covered fifteen acres of land. They manufactured railway carriages, railway wagons and tramcars for export to India, South America and the British Colonies. In the 1880s over 800 people were employed there. In 1902 it merged with five other wagon works, and it closed in 1908. The former railway line between Lancaster and Yorkshire passed by their works.

Many pupils now pass through Ripley St Thomas School, and have done since 1966. The school began its life as Ripley Hospital (28607, page 69), which was built between 1854 and 1864 (a chapel designed by Paley & Austin was added in 1888) by Mrs Julia Ripley following the death of her husband, Thomas. He was a Lancaster man who had prospered as a merchant in Liverpool, and had intended to endow the town with a large school. The school was originally an orphanage, and provided education and maintenance for boys and girls from a radius of fifteen miles from Lancaster or seven miles from Liverpool. The school still has very strong links with the Church of England, but it is inter-denominational.

Telephone : Lancaster **4334** (3 lines)

Telegrams : " Standfast Phone Lancaster "

●

STANDFAST

Dyers & Printers Limited
LANCASTER

BLEACHERS, MERCERISERS, DYERS AND PRINTERS OF HIGH CLASS COTTON AND RAYON GOODS BOTH CLOTH AND YARN

Pioneers and Specialists in
FAST DYES

Licensers of the Standfast (Reg. Trade Mark) Patent Molten Metal Dyeing Process

●

Specialists in
REVERSIBLE FAST PRINTS

STANDFAST ADVERTISEMENT ZZZ00457

Standfast Dyers & Printers Ltd took over the wagon works until they moved further along Caton Road.

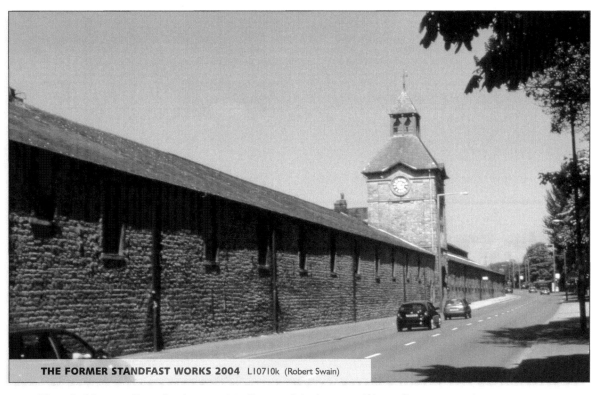

THE FORMER STANDFAST WORKS 2004 L10710k (Robert Swain)

These buildings on Caton Road were originally part of the Lancaster Wagon Company premises.

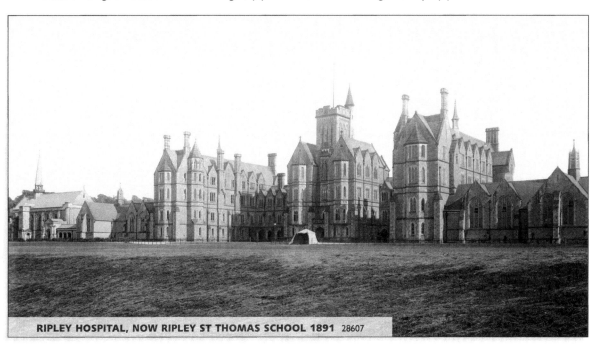

RIPLEY HOSPITAL, NOW RIPLEY ST THOMAS SCHOOL 1891 28607

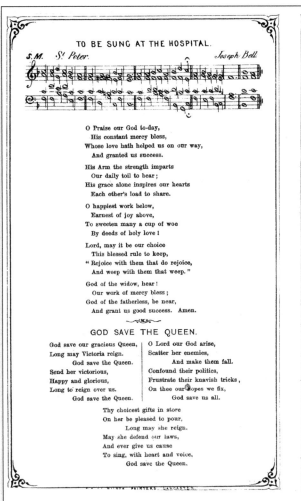

OFFICIAL PROGRAMME, OPENING OF RIPLEY'S HOSPITAL 1864 ZZZ00472 (Lancaster Library)

Fact File

The opening of Ripley Hospital on 3 November 1864 was a colourful occasion. A procession of 7,000 wound its way from the Town Hall in Market Square round Market Street, Castle Hill, and Church Street, then through Dalton Square and Brock Street and on to the Hospital. Flags were flying from the buildings of Lancaster. Mrs Ripley was greeted with applause when she arrived on the platform ready for the opening by the Bishop of Manchester.

There were lighter moments during the 19th century. One of these took place on 21 September 1861, and was reported in the Lancaster Guardian. A man styling himself 'the English Blondin' after a famous tightrope walker had announced his intention to cross the Lune by way of a tightrope at an elevation of 15 feet. A crowd of four or five thousand people lined both the St George's Quay and the Skerton sides of the river for the event. On the quay side, the rope was fastened to 'a ships fastener', and at the Skerton side it was supported by triangles. To prevent any considerable deflection or oscillation of the rope, guy lines were attached at various stages and were firmly held by people in boats, purposely engaged for the event. 'At a few minutes to seven in the evening, the English Blondin commenced his journey, with the aid of a long balancing pole. He proceeded along the rope steadily but not swiftly and about half way knelt and lay along the rope'. On reaching Skerton, he received warm applause, and made a speech from his rope. 'From the quayside he was barely discernible as it was nearly dark, but he returned safely and received a weighty copper collection'.

In 1881 Gillow's moved from Castle Hill and Green Ayre to extensive new premises in North Road, which were their showrooms, whilst behind were the workshops fronting onto St Leonardgate. No longer were there any members of the Gillow family in the business - the last Gillow had retired from the firm in 1830.

The laying of the foundation stone for the Royal Albert Hospital on 17 June 1868 (ZZZ00471, below) was another big occasion

ROYAL ALBERT ASYLUM FOR IDIOTS AND IMBECILES,
AT LANCASTER,
FOUNDATION STONE LAID JUNE 17TH, 1868,
BY THE EARL OF ZETLAND, K.T.,
MOST WORSHIPFUL GRAND MASTER OF THE FREEMASONS OF ENGLAND.

LANCASTER GAZETTE SUPPLEMENT: THE LAYING OF THE ROYAL ALBERT ASYLUM FOUNDATION STONE 1868

ZZZ00471 (Lancaster Library)

for Lancaster; the Mayor had proclaimed that no vehicle could drive through the streets that were to be used for the procession that afternoon. The Rifle Volunteers assembled in Market Square, the Artillery Corps in New Street and the Friendly Societies in Church Street, while the Mayor, the Corporation, the clergy, other officials and the public assembled at the Town Hall. Special trains had been laid on to bring in between eight and nine thousand visitors from the seven northern counties of England, the area for which the hospital was being built.

The hospital came about through a Dr Edward de Vitre, visiting physician at the County Lunatic Asylum, later to become part of the Moor Hospital. The doctor had arrived

from Scotland in 1832; he soon realised that there were different types of mental health problems, and worked to bring about a change in people's attitudes. James Brunton, a local Quaker, appreciated that provision should be made for the mentally impaired, and made the donation of £2,000 that set the work in motion to start fund-raising for the hospital. Royal patronage started with Queen Victoria, who gave 100 guineas (£105) to the fund; her successors followed her example. Major donors over the years included Lord Ashton and in particular Thomas Storey, below, who paid for the Storey Home for Feeble-minded Girls.

The first patients admitted at the new hospital arrived in December 1870. At first,

SIR THOMAS STOREY, FROM LANCASTER GUARDIAN REPORT ON THE STOREY HOME ZZZ00469 (Lancaster Library)

THE ROYAL ALBERT ASYLUM 1891 50060

the Royal Albert (seen above) was a voluntary hospital. Its aim was to train young people to be able to live normal lives rather than to keep them there permanently. Many of the patients were able to return to outside lives over the years; in 1909, of 662 patients, 504 had been there for less than ten years. Patients learned various skills over the years, and worked on the farm attached to the hospital. In later years, one patient became such an expert on the electric wiring of the buildings that he was consulted by North Western Electricity Board employees when they were called on to work there.

Dr de Vitre was chairman of the Central Committee of the hospital until his death in 1878. He had also been Physician to the Dispensary, having resigned from that post in 1840. During his time in Lancaster he had twice been Mayor; he had also been a Port Commissioner, and he had various other interests in the town. His name lives on in De Vitre Street, terraced houses by the former Albion Mill (L10711k), and De Vitre Cottages, a terrace close to the Royal Albert.

In 1833 the People's Dispensary and the House of Recovery were merged and moved to new premises on Thurnham Street, now known as Owen House. As Lancaster continued to expand, the need for the

DE VITRE STREET 2004 LI071lk (Robert Swain)

provision of a new infirmary grew. Land was found on Ashton Road, and in 1888 the site was purchased for £2,741. Mr Paley of Paley & Austin was appointed as architect, and work began. Funds were raised, in particular £6,300 from James Williamson, who laid the foundation stone on 12 July 1893.

On 24 March 1896 the Duke and Duchess of York (the future George V and Queen Mary) came to formally open the Infirmary, using a golden key to open the main door (see page 75). After declaring it open, the Duke announced that Queen Victoria, his grandmother, was pleased that the institution

'be known as the Royal Lancaster Infirmary'.

The decline in Lancaster's fortunes in the early years of the century meant that there was no need for more housing, so the Georgian buildings (of which several survive) were retained. Planned development did not take place, and the town centre consisted of the cramped courts and yards, the business premises and the houses of merchants and professional people. Only the very rich lived in large detached residences, often beyond the boundaries of the town as they then were, which did not then include Skerton or Scotforth. Some large houses were in the

THE INFIRMARY 1896 37380

Whilst these buildings still stand, later buildings make this view towards the main entrance (by the trees on the right) no longer possible.

THE OPENING OF THE ROYAL LANCASTER INFIRMARY 1896 ZZZ00466 (Lancaster Library)

town, such as Parkfield and Greaves House, both of which had extensive grounds.

From the 1840s, residential Lancaster started to be developed. Much of this housing was terraced. Building took place wherever there was available land. In George Street, Thurnham Street and Marton Street, small houses were built tightly packed together on land sold by G B H Marton in 1844.

The earliest estate to be built, and also the largest, was Freehold, which was not constructed for commercial reasons, but for national political reasons. In the mid 1800s the right to vote was based on property ownership, which had to be worth more than two pounds annually. This law was particularly likely to increase the Liberal vote. The area of 38 acres was purchased for £6,500 in 1852 and parcelled into 364 plots. So as to qualify under the £2 rule, the plots were large and had very long gardens, something different from elsewhere in Lancaster. The estate is on a grid pattern, with Rydal Road, Dalton Road and Borrowdale Road being crossed by Derwent Road, Windermere Road, Grasmere Road and Ullswater Road. Dalton Road has the sides of houses and their long gardens.

Freehold developed slowly because of the costs involved. Some plots were subdivided, and terraces were built on others. There were not enough people in the town sufficiently wealthy to buy plots outright, and by 1861 there were only 30 owners. The estate is built on a hillside, with the larger houses up the hill and the smaller ones below.

Politics in Lancaster until later in the 1800s were very different from today, as the corrupt practices during the election of 1865 show. Acts had been passed to bring about a fairer, less corrupt, system of election. At that time, Barrow-in-Furness was a very new town, and had no parliamentary representation. Schneider, the ore merchant and industrialist so eminent in that new town, wanted 'a nice little seat in Parliament', but knew that there was no immediate prospect of Barrow obtaining representation. On the death of Samuel Gregson, one of Lancaster's two MPs, he took his place unopposed. However, only a few months later in July 1865 there was a General Election. Schneider, a Liberal, was opposed by Edward Lawrence, the Mayor of Liverpool, a Conservative.

The business of gaining votes took place in the pubs, not at the hustings. In the Conservative-supporting Lancaster Gazette of 1 July it was reported that 'nearly all the public houses' in the town were in the service of the Liberals. Schneider himself was to write that Lancaster was 'fearfully corrupt'. Towards the date of the election it was reported that votes were costing nearly £10 each, with both parties paying out large sums. Schneider and Fenwick, the other Liberal candidate, narrowly won the two Lancaster seats. At the subsequent enquiry, the Commissioners concluded that Schneider and Fenwick had spent between them over £7,400, most of which had been converted to drink for the freemen of Lancaster. Of 1,408 electors, 843 had received inducements for their votes. Political issues appear to have received little consideration.

In September 1866 Lancaster's Shire Hall saw a long examination by the Royal Commissioners, where many witnesses admitted to being bribed and specified the amounts of money they had received. As a result of the enquiry, the Commissioners ordered Schneider and Fenwick to be unseated. Following the election, in the 1867 Reform Bill it was provided that Lancaster, along with Yarmouth, Reigate and Totnes, were disfranchised. It only regained the right to parliamentary representation from 1885, when seats had been redistributed and the constituency then included much of Lonsdale South of the Sands and part of Amounderness. James Williamson was the first MP to be elected.

To the Right Honourable W. E. Gladstone, M.P.,
First Lord of the Treasury.

The Respectful Memorial of the Mayor, Aldermen, and Burgesses of the Borough of Lancaster in Council Assembled.

Sheweth,

That at the Election of Members to serve in Parliament for the Borough of Lancaster in the Year 1865, a portion of the Constituency was guilty of corrupt practices; and in consequence the Borough, by the Act of 30 and 31 Victoria, chapter 102, was deprived of its Parliamentary representatives.

That your Memorialists feel the disgrace and disadvantage of this Disfranchisement, and respectfully submit the following reasons for the restoration of the Franchise which the Town so long possessed :—

1.—Lancaster is the Capital of the Duchy and County Palatine from which Her Majesty the Queen derives one of Her ancient Titles. It is one of the oldest towns in the Kingdom. It received a Charter from King John (when Earl of Moreton) in the year 1193, and it was one of the four Boroughs in Lancashire which in the thirteenth Century were required to return Burgesses to Parliament. From that date, until the Year 1866, it had been represented by two Members in the House of Commons; and it is proud of its participation in the history of the country. Whilst many old Boroughs have declined, Lancaster has made steady progress; and during the last twenty years, it has greatly advanced in population, wealth, and industrial enterprise. In its Schools, Charities, Public Institutions, and other evidences of a thriving and intelligent community, Lancaster will favourably compare with other Boroughs of similar extent, and there is every reason to believe that it will continue to exhibit the same ratio of prosperity and importance which has marked the latest period of its history. Your Memorialists, therefore, whilst pleading for the restoration of the privilege which had been enjoyed for upwards of six hundred years, can also point to those signs of progress which are now considered necessary to entitle a town to Parliamentary representation.

2.—The number of pure Electors of the Borough of Lancaster at the time of its disfranchisement was larger than the entire Constituency of each of seventy English represented Boroughs. Those Electors were deprived of their privileges although guiltless of Electoral corruption; and the still larger number of inhabitants who would have been entitled to the franchise under the Reform Bill of 1867 are innocently suffering the same punishment.

3.—The last Election for Lancaster took place upwards of nineteen years ago, and since then the persons scheduled as guilty of corrupt practices have been reduced more than three-fourths in number by death or removal.

4.—It is submitted that it has not been the practice of Parliament permanently to disfranchise Boroughs of the importance of Lancaster. Instances might be cited of other places, more recently convicted of corrupt practices, which were not disfranchised, but a punishment inflicted less severe than Lancaster has already endured; yet in these cases the offences were committed under more stringent provisions than were in force in 1865.

5.—The boundary of the Borough was fixed by the Reform Bill of 1832. Since that time the population has almost doubled, and its immediate suburbs have become important and populous. Within a short distance, and intimately connected with it, are several considerable and rapidly increasing places contributing materially to the importance of the district of which Lancaster is the centre. The population of the Lancaster Registration District, according to the census of 1881, was over 40,000, and the value of the rateable property in Lancaster alone has more than doubled during the last nineteen years, and shews, since the last assessment, a greater increase than almost any other Borough in the County.

Your Memorialists earnestly pray that these facts may be taken into favorable consideration, with a view to the restoration to Lancaster of its ancient right to representation in the House of Commons.

Given under the Common Seal of the Borough of Lancaster, this Ninth day of October, 1884.

SAMUEL J. HARRIS,
MAYOR.

(L. S.)

LETTER TO GLADSTONE FROM THE MAYOR OF LANCASTER 1884 ZZZ00476 (Lancaster Library)

PARLIAMENTARY ELECTION
1895.

LANCASTER DIVISION.

LANCASTER POLLING DISTRICT.
John O'Gaunt Ward.

POLLING DAY.

FRIDAY, JULY 19TH, 1895,
From 8 a.m. to 8 p.m.

Name *R. O. Goad,*

Number on Register M. *4111*

YOUR POLLING PLACE IS

No. 2.—ST. THOMAS' SCHOOL, LANCASTER.

NOTE.—After voting please deliver this Card to Mr. Leadam's messenger waiting outside the Polling Station, or at the Committee Room.

Printed by EATON & BULFIELD, King Street, Lancaster.
Published by W. TILLY, Election Agent, 10, Sun Street, Lancaster

(OVER

A POLLING CARD FROM THE 1895 PARLIAMENTARY ELECTION ZZZ00475 (Lancaster Library)

Lancaster had been disenfranchised after the corrupt election of 1865. This letter pleads for Lancaster to again be represented in the House of Commons.

THE CASTLE, THE INTERIOR OF THE SHIRE HALL 1927 80513

THE CASTLE, THE SHIELDS 1936 87343

In the Shire Hall hang the shields of the monarchs, the Constables of the Castle and the High Sheriffs of Lancashire.

Much of Lancaster's residential development took place from the 1870s, thanks to the expansion of Williamson's and Storey Bros. That decade saw the Marsh estate and the Dry Dock estate both being built close by the mills. They were built just as housing, and contained no business premises other than some shops. These estates were all terraced.

Victorian terraces were not built just for factory employees. One terrace on South Road, Spring Bank, was in 1901 occupied by professional people, who included an architect. The terraces were built where there was some spare land, which results in their being interestingly varied. For example, Vicarage Terrace, off St George's Quay, has only four houses.

The main road layout of Lancaster is not much changed since the time that Skerton Bridge was built. However, in the late 1800s it became necessary to broaden some of the streets and start the clearance of some slum property. China Lane, now China Street, was only eight feet wide at its junction with Church Street. Whilst some original frontage remains on the east side of China Street, the west side is much changed owing to its widening in 1895. Earlier, in 1876, medieval cottages in front of the castle gateway were purchased as the result of a publicity campaign and demolished to make the grassy area we have today.

PORTLAND STREET, EAST SIDE 2004 L10712k (Robert Swain)

MOORLANDS ESTATE AND ST PETER'S CATHEDRAL FROM LANCASTER PRIORY 2004 L10714k (Robert Swain)

BOWERHAM TERRACE 2004 L10713k (Robert Swain)

CHINA STREET c1955 L10052

Some of the fronts of the original buildings of China Street are on the left. Ahead, where King Street bends round to the left, stands the King's Arms Hotel.

A.A. Lancaster 2451/2 R.A.C.

ROYAL KING'S ARMS HOTEL

Corner of Market Street and Meeting House Lane
(next to the G.P.O.)

LANCASTER'S LEADING HOTEL

Fully licensed, 60 bedrooms, all with h. and c., and some with telephones, large dining room, lift to all floors, T.V., Ballroom, 2 minutes walk to Railway and Bus Stations, in sight of the Castle

ENQUIRIES FOR WEDDINGS, BANQUETS, DANCES, MEETINGS, EXTENDED TOURS
ETC. WILL BE WELCOMED BY THE MANAGER

**ADVERTISEMENT FOR THE
ROYAL KING'S ARMS HOTEL** ZZZ00461

Fact File

The Royal King's Arms Hotel replaced an old coaching inn, the premier inn in the town for many years, which was demolished in 1879. It was a terminus for the Over Sands coach route between Lancaster and Ulverston, which crossed the sands of Morecambe Bay. Between 1856 and 1877 the landlord was Joseph Sly; he regularly sent hampers of game to Charles Dickens, who had a great affection for the inn.

A major change was the establishment of a new covered market. In 1878 the Corporation looked at the design of Ulverston Market, with a view to having a covered market of their own. Progress was slow, as the Lancaster Guardian reported, and work did not begin until 16 September 1879, when the Mayor, accompanied by the Corporation, walked to the site to lay the foundation stone. In May 1880 the building was ready for use, and it was opened with the usual formal ceremony by the Mayor, with a crowd of around five or six thousand people watching.

CHAPTER FOUR

THE TWENTIETH CENTURY

THE TOWN HALL 1912 64215p

LORD ASHTON felt that Lancaster needed new and larger municipal buildings, and offered to provide them in 1904. Work on the present Town Hall (above) started in 1906, with E W Mountford of London as the architect. Waring & Gillow provided the internal woodwork and carvings, including the beautifully counterbalanced screens that can be raised or lowered to adjust the size of the banqueting hall overlooking Dalton Square. The Town Hall houses the Ashton Hall, venue for many events in the town. Dalton Square (page 86) was part of the scheme, including the bronze statue of Queen Victoria, which was originally intended for

Covell Cross was erected in 1902 to commemorate the coronation of Edward VII. It stands on the site of an earlier cross.

COVELL CROSS 2004 L10715k (Robert Swain)

Williamson Park. The whole scheme cost £155,000 and was officially opened by Lord Ashton on 27 December 1909. All the Lancaster schoolchildren were brought to see the buildings.

Williamson Park continued to be developed by Lord Ashton. In 1904 he had the original rustic bridge replaced by the stone bridge; also, a bandstand was constructed and six shelters were built around the park. The Palm House, now the butterfly house, was built. The major building erected at this time was the Ashton Memorial (64220), said to be in memory of Jessie, his second wife, who died in 1904. Sir John Belcher, a London

THE TOWN HALL

The Town Hall occupies the site of two fine old Georgian houses. Within are the town's silver, an extending circular Gillow table, and one of the few portraits of Lord Ashton. The portrait can have a disturbing effect on people, particularly at night, as it appears to be always facing the viewer regardless of where he or she is standing. The old Magistrates' Court is here, and so are the cells – the murderer Dr Buck Ruxton was held in one of them. All of these things can be seen when taking a conducted tour.

THE TOWN HALL 1912 64218

architect, was commissioned to design the memorial; it was originally to have been built in stone, but the specification was changed to brick, steel joists, concrete infill and stone cladding, an experimental technique that was to lead to very serious problems in the 1980s. Gillow's carried out the contract for the work, which began in 1907. The memorial stands 150 feet high, a prominent landmark around Lancaster – it is a sign to many motorists on the M6 that they are nearing home.

By 1909 Lord Ashton was known as 'the linoleum king'. Two years later it was said that Williamson & Sons employed nearly a quarter of Lancaster's working men, and possibly a similar proportion of women and children.

People were generally engaged at the factory gates as required. Discipline was strict, as was necessary at a site where inflammable materials were used. Dismissible offences included carrying matches onto the site, as well as bad time-keeping and drunkenness. Also, it was locally believed that a person's politics could affect his or her prospects. However, a job at Williamson's was looked upon as a job for life, as long as the rules were observed.

Pay was not high, but early in the century it was above the local labouring rates. Lord Ashton did not appreciate attempts by the Independent Labour Party to unionise the firm's general workers, considering his own

THE MEMORIAL GARDENS, DALTON SQUARE c1955 L10046

Buses passed round Dalton Square on their way to the south. The County Cinema is on the right.

THE ASHTON MEMORIAL 1912 64220

paternalism adequate; indeed, the ILP did not succeed until after his death. However, its actions and unrest amongst the workforce were probably what led to Lord Ashton ceasing to make gifts to the town from 1911 and to live mainly in St Anne's.

To the right of the Old Town Hall in Market Square, where the library is now, was Lancaster's first telephone exchange (with the masts on top, in the centre of 50057, page 88). Beside it were the police station and the fire station. The next fire station was located under the present Town Hall; then it was moved to the modern building in Cable Street.

October 1935 saw Lancaster hit the headlines following the discovery of two bodies at Gardenholme Linn, near Moffat in Dumfriesshire. The murderer had been to considerable trouble to disfigure the bodies to try to prevent their identification, and had wrapped the remains in various articles including newspapers. The bodies were so disfigured that at first it was thought that they were of a man and a woman. One newspaper wrapping had a headline referring to '...ambe's Carnival Queen ..rowned', with a photograph of a girl wearing a crown. This turned out to be from a special edition of only 3,700 copies of a newspaper distributed in Lancaster and Morecambe.

The Lancaster police were contacted. At the time they were involved with the disappearance of Isabella Ruxton and her

THE OLD TOWN HALL 1903 50057

maid, Mary Jane Rogerson, from their house in Dalton Square three weeks earlier. Mrs Ruxton, as she was known, was the common-law wife of Dr Buck Ruxton, originally from India but practising in Lancaster. The couple had three children. Their relationship was stormy, and it was locally alleged that Mrs Ruxton had a number of men 'friends'.

Dr Ruxton gave a number of explanations as to why the two women had gone missing during the days after their disappearance. It subsequently transpired that he had murdered his wife in a fit of passion; Mary Rogerson had apparently witnessed the murder, and so she was killed too as a precaution. The bodies were cut up in the bath before being wrapped up and taken by car to where they

were discovered. Pioneering forensic work was involved in the case, particularly the matching of the skulls to photographs of the victims, which proved their identity.

Locally, Dr Ruxton was well liked and respected, and a petition raised 6,000 signatures in his support. It is often said that he would not have received the death sentence if he had not killed Mary Rogerson as well as his wife.

Storey Brothers had become a limited company by the beginning of the 20th century, but it was still a family-run business and had a good relationship with its employees. On many occasions when an employee retired or a pensioner died, the firm received a letter of thanks for the kindness of the company from

QUEEN VICTORIA MONUMENT 1912 64217p

Dr Ruxton's house in Dalton Square is immediately to the left of the monument.

**PALATINE HALL, THE FORMER COUNTY CINEMA, AND
DR RUXTON'S HOUSE 2004** L10716k (Robert Swain)

either the employee or his or her family. During the First World War the company manufactured shells, having purchased machinery especially for this purpose. This did not happen during the Second World War, when vast quantities of black-out materials, tarpaulins and other similar goods were produced.

In the 1930s, it was first proposed (probably by Alderman Parr) that Lancaster should be elevated to the status of city. Confidential representations were started in December 1936;

THE KING'S OWN ROYAL REGIMENT

Following the reorganisation of the army by Edward Cardwell, Secretary of State for War, after the disastrous Crimean War, the King's Own Royal Regiment was allocated to Lancaster; its recruiting area stretched from Fleetwood to Barrow and Coniston. In 1873, land was purchased from the Bowerham Estate for the building of a new barracks, which were first occupied in 1880. The barracks continued in use until 1959. In 1903, a memorial chapel was built on the north side of Lancaster Priory Church in memory of those from the regiment who lost their lives in the South African campaign of 1899-1902. Paley & Austin were the architects and another local firm, Shrigley & Hunt, provided much of the stained glass. The chapel houses the colourful banners of the regiment and commemorates the two World Wars.

THE PARISH CHURCH, THE KING'S OWN MEMORIAL CHAPEL 1927 80527

the outcome was that on the evening of the coronation of George VI and Queen Elizabeth in May 1937, the Town Clerk reported to the city that the king, on the recommendation of the Secretary of State, 'has been graciously pleased on the occasion of His Coronation to raise the Borough of Lancaster to the title and dignity of a City'. Letters Patent were about to confirm the Great Seal. The Mayor sent a telegram of thanks and congratulated Their Majesties on their coronation.

Fact File

No 1 High Street was the birthplace of the poet Laurence Binyon in August 1869. The first five years of his life were spent in the Lancaster area, which he always remembered. Although he did not consider it his best poem, Binyon is chiefly remembered for the poem 'For the Fallen' which was written very early during the First World War. The words of the fourth verse appear on many war memorials and are spoken at remembrance services: 'They shall grow not old, as we that are left grow old ......'

The city has long provided various forms of relaxation. The cinemas and the theatre played a large part in the lives of Lancastrians for much of the 20th century, particularly until the 1960s. Storeys' Works Band, which was founded in 1946, became well known around the district, performing at many venues over the years, and won their section of the Daily Herald National Brass Band Championship in 1948. The Lancaster Canal (see page 92) changed from commercial use to leisure use. The last commercial traffic on it was a cargo of coal carried to White Cross Mills in 1947.

LANCASTER'S CINEMAS

Besides buildings converted for use as cinemas at some stage, such as Palatine Hall, the Grand Theatre and the Duke's Playhouse (formerly St Anne's Church), Lancaster had five purpose-built cinemas. In Market Street was the Palladium, now used by W H Smith. Lower Church Street had the Rex, which was demolished to make way for the shopping precinct. Dalton Square had the Union and the Palace, which was regularly used by the murderer Dr Ruxton. The Odeon, opened in 1936, was looked on as the 'posh' one, as it had the nicest seats and the best films. More recently called the Regal, it closed its doors in 2006, just before the opening of a new six-screen Vue multiplex in Church Street with 1,546 seats

KING STREET c1955 L10043

Lancaster never reached the very top in sport, but it has long had both a cricket club and a football field. Giant Axe Field (below) has housed both football and cricket over the years, and is home to Lancaster City Football Club; the Lancaster Cricket Club's home is on Lune Road. The River Lune has also played its part with the John o'Gaunt Rowing Club.

The 20th century saw big changes for Gillow's. By 1900 they had become associated with Waring, a Liverpool firm,

GIANT AXE FIELD 1918 68330

BRIDGES OF THE LANCASTER CANAL

In this photograph, a young angler concentrates on watching his float by Haverbreaks Bridge. Many of the bridges on the Lancaster Canal are called 'Rennie Standards': they are all built to a basic design by John Rennie. However, they are probably all slightly different. For instance, this one has no keystone in the arch. The next one on towards Lancaster is a converted ship's gangway. The bridge by the canal basins is a turnover bridge, so designed that horses could be backed over it without being detached from their boats and then continue on their way along the towpath on the other side of the canal.

THE CANAL 1918 68332

and became Waring & Gillow. They were then contracted to do work on many of the great liners, such as the 'Empress of Britain' and the 'Queen Mary'. During the Second World War, production was given over to building Horsa gliders and tentage. One local man felt nervous on his way to Arnhem - until he realised that he was in a Gillow glider. Another local man was injured in Italy, and

when he came to in a tent, the first thing he saw was the Waring & Gillow name.

In later years, work carried out by them included the coronation stools, seating for the House of Commons, and work in the Liverpool cathedrals and in many town halls, including Lancaster's. A takeover in 1961 saw the closure of the works, which had trained many excellent craftsmen over the years.

THE CANAL 2004 L10717k (Robert Swain)

The former White Cross Mills flank the Lancaster Canal at White Cross.

Several old buildings and streets were demolished in the 1960s with the development of the shopping precinct around St Nicholas Arcades and Arndale House. This, as in most towns, was done in the belief by the authorities that the new style was better; but the result was that some areas lost their character, such as St Nicolas Street, most of which was lost, and Common Garden Street. Arndale House was built around the covered market hall, which was retained, and fronted onto both King Street and Common Garden Street. At that time, Gillinson's Hospital, eight houses for unmarried women, was demolished, along with several popular, long-established shops and a café. By the end of the century, the new developments were looking quite out of place and scruffy. In the 1990s, St Nicholas Arcades was largely rebuilt, and is now more in keeping with the appearance of its surroundings.

In the 1960s and 1970s a number of terraced streets were demolished ready for building the Eastern Relief Road round the eastern side of the town centre, near the canal. The road was not built and probably never will be, particularly in view of recent building works.

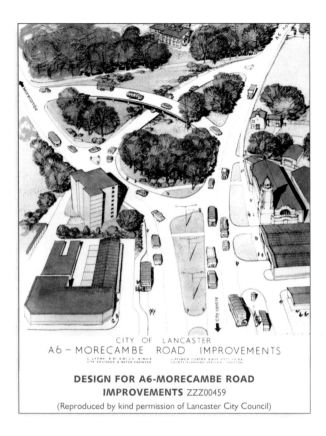

CITY OF LANCASTER
A6 – MORECAMBE ROAD IMPROVEMENTS

DESIGN FOR A6-MORECAMBE ROAD IMPROVEMENTS ZZZ00459
(Reproduced by kind permission of Lancaster City Council)

It was at the time of the redevelopment of the city centre that Lancaster's industries started to close down, including those on Caton Road; Lansil closing in 1980. Home improvements following the war had increased the demand for floor and wall coverings. However, changes in ownerships of the manufacturing firms and changes in technology led to the first redundancies. The demand for oilcloth and coated fabrics led to Williamson's merging with their former rivals, Nairns of Kirkcaldy, and linoleum manufacture was transferred to Scotland. Since that time, the Lune Mills continued to operate for a number of years, but they have now all closed, and most of the buildings have either been demolished or are awaiting demolition. By May 1985 the once vast workforce had been reduced to 550. Similarly, Storey Bros was taken over by Turner & Newall in 1977 and subsequently sold, but many of the buildings at White Cross remain as various business and other units.

In the city centre, most of the family-run businesses have closed, including the grocers J R & W Bell and T D Smith - the latter hung on until 1981 in Dalton Square. No longer does the Lancaster and District Co-operative Society Ltd have premises occupying an extensive block between New Street, Church Street and Market Square; only the frontage has been retained, and it is now part of Woolworth's and other businesses.

LANCASTER CO-OP ADVERTISEMENT ZZZ00455
(Reproduced by kind permission of Lancaster City Council)

SHOPS ON PENNY STREET

Penny Street has been a main street since the Romans came. The buildings along it were constructed of wood and burned down at various times. The street housed a very wide variety of private shops along its length. In this photograph, we see Alan Dent on the left, which was well known for cycles, and provided bed and breakfast for cyclists. Chris Willan on the right had a variety of shops, including a toyshop. The shop on the right was at one time his electrical shop, which not only sold electrical goods but also rented out televisions. A number of the proprietors of the shops lived above their premises. Now, Lancaster has very many fewer private traders.

PENNY STREET c1950 L10044

People scurrying home on Monday, 8 October 1984 were not aware of the fire breaking out in the covered market. It became a huge fire lighting up the sky of the centre of Lancaster, and completely destroyed the building and the heart of the city. A number of the Arndale House shops were burned out as well. A temporary market hall was re-opened on the site in December, but something permanent had to be done.

Much discussion and controversy over the covered market and its future site and ownership took place over the following years. The city was told that the market might not be on its original site, or not all on ground level. The market traders and others argued against this as not being appropriate; the market had occupied a position which drew people through it when passing from one street to another. However, the eventual

REDDROP'S

Reddrop's on the right was a well-known draper's. In the 1940s, girls left school to work there. They were each supplied with a black dress, and were paid half a crown (12½ pence) a week, and a 6-day week, at that! Besides being a draper's, Reddrop's added a travel agency to the business; this continued in Ffrances Passage after the drapery closed. The Cheapside shop became Carline's, a grocer's, before the premises were demolished. Now, the site is one entrance to St Nicholas Arcades.

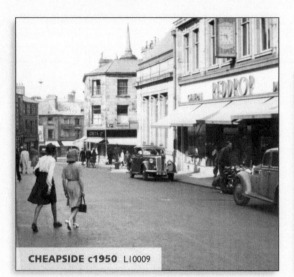

CHEAPSIDE c1950 L10009

REDDROP AND COMPANY LTD.

HAVE PLEASURE IN PLACING AT YOUR DISPOSAL THEIR

World Travel Service

Telephone
LANCASTER 3624

Address
CHEAPSIDE & CHURCH STREET

Member of A.B.T.A.   No Booking Fees

REDDROP & CO LTD ADVERTISEMENT
ZZZ00460

decision went against these arguments, with the result that the market is now on the corner of King Street and Common Garden Street and is on two levels, both points being to its detriment. The fish market was built at the sunniest end instead of at a cooler part, as was the case with the old market.

Whilst the market was being rebuilt, a large part of the bus station was covered over to house the stalls temporarily, and several of the bus stops were moved to uncovered locations nearby, leading to problems in bad weather and complaints from passengers.

During the 20th century there were major changes at Lancaster Castle. The numbers of prisoners had fallen considerably, and owing to the opening of courts in Manchester and Liverpool, fewer people were held awaiting trial. Thomas Rawcliffe was the last person to be hanged in Lancaster on 15 November 1910. In 1916 it was decided to close the prison; from then on, it was used for various purposes, first as a training school for policemen, and then during the Second World War as an Air

LANCASTER MARKET 2004 L10718k (Robert Swain)

Raid Patrol depot. In 1955 the prison was again opened, but it is at present intended that it will be closed when the present lease runs out.

It was 1982 when work started on converting the Custom House into the Maritime Museum. On the ground floor an electricity sub-station from the 1930s had to be removed. Also, the building had been altered for use by a local theatre group. During the conversion, a staircase was inserted so that for the first time both floors could be reached internally. However, this was not the end. Later, much of the adjoining warehouse became free, and it was converted to house more exhibitions and a café, making the building as it is today.

THE MARITIME MUSEUM (THE FORMER CUSTOM HOUSE AND A WAREHOUSE) 2004 L10719k (Robert Swain)

THE LADIES' WALK c1910 L10025

THE FIFTEENTH LANCASTER EASTER

MARITIME FESTIVAL

18th – 21st April 2003
(Good Friday to Easter Monday)

The City's four day celebration of Sea Songs, Shanties & Matters Maritime

Featuring the world's biggest gathering of sea song & shanty singers, supported by a wide array of Maritime themed entertainments including a *Grand Celebration* of Mr Punch & his Wife Judy!

PROGRAMME *of* EVENTS

MARITIME FESTIVAL POSTER 2003 ZZZ00452 (Lancaster City Council)

The Maritime Festival at Easter centres on the Maritime Museum, and many of the events take place round it and along St George's Quay.

During the 20th century, the Royal Lancaster Infirmary has expanded considerably, taking up much of the land close by. It and the Nuffield Hospital provide health care for many miles around. Lancaster used to have an isolation hospital at the very end of St

George's Quay; it opened in 1881 following an outbreak of smallpox around the Thurnham Street infirmary. It remained in use as a hospital until 1934, when the now demolished Beaumont Hospital was opened.

The isolation hospital was the scene of drama on 29 October 1927, the start of a week of high tides and heavy rains. The first warning the patients in the hospital had of what was to come was from the whistling of the wind as a hurricane approached. The Lune came over the small embankment, and an estimated 30 million gallons of water flooded the area. In the hospital grounds were wooden shelters, and here three patients drowned. The hospital could only be reached by boat or by men wading. The dispensary was flooded, the lights failed, and the patients had to be carried upstairs by helpers. The licensee of the Blue Anchor (on the quay) showed great valour that night, and it was suggested that he receive a Royal Humane Society award. Subsequently, the coroner commented on the bravery of all those people who had helped during the night.

One of the patients, five-year old Doris Redmayne who had diphtheria, told of how the beds were afloat. After the tide had gone down, a farmer on the Marsh, William Whitaker, came and took the patients to safety by horse and a flat cart. During the night he had lost ninety sheep and hay valued at about £120. Fortunately, his mare had been able to lead her foal to safety.

In 1937 Bridge Lane was re-aligned and widened from its junction with Church Street to make a new road leading down to the bus station, which was then built. This involved the demolition of much property between Cable Street and Damside Street.

One of the main changes to the roads in the 20th century was at the Ladies' Walk (page 98), which ran from the end of Skerton Bridge, along what is now Kingsway, to join up with Caton Road close to the Lancaster Wagon Co Ltd factory. It is said that before the Dissolution of the Monasteries the nuns walked here, and it remained a pleasant, tree-lined walk until the present Caton Road was built - it occupies much of the site of the Ladies' Walk. Before that, Caton Road, part of the one-way system, was the road from the town centre to Caton; it replaced Bulk Road, which was once known as Old Caton Road.

However, there was a proposed major change to the junction of the A6 and Morecambe Road at Skerton in the 1960s, a time when much of old Skerton was demolished and the flats built. If the road change had gone ahead, the corner of Ryelands Park would have been crossed by two sections of road, one passing over the other, and reaching nearly to Ryelands House.

Bailrigg was a hamlet within the township of Scotforth. Sir Thomas Storey bought the estate at Bailrigg in 1887, and the house was completed in 1898. Later, it was sold to the Barton-Townley family. Although the estate lies just outside the old city boundary, it has an important role in Lancaster's story as the future site for Lancaster University.

Seven new universities were to be built in the 1960s, one of which was to be in the north-west of England. Originally, a number of places put in applications for this university, but by 21 April 1961 the competition had dropped down to just two, Blackpool and Lancaster - Lytham St Anne's had decided to withdraw its claim earlier in the week.

Mr J A Waddell, the Town Clerk of Lancaster, did much work to promote Lancaster's case, and it was he who led the team presenting it to an all-important committee meeting in Preston on that day. They knew that they had to show to the University Grants Committee that the area had a cultural background, proximity to learned institutions, housing and facilities for university staff, local interest, and a site of 200 acres. Before attending the meeting, Mr Waddell had said, 'I can only hope that when they see what we have to offer they will be impressed in our favour'. Earlier, he had realised that pushing the case for the university to be sited at the Royal Albert Hospital could spoil Lancaster's chances, and had approached the Barton-Townley family to see if they

A cordial invitation is extended to

MR. AND MRS. J. WELCH

to be present at a special Service in

The Priory and Parish Church of St. Mary, Lancaster,

on Friday, 9th October, 1964, at 11 a.m.

to mark the commencement of the first academic session of

The University of Lancaster

and of

S. Martin's College of Education, Lancaster.

R.S.V.P. to the Secretary of the University,
The University of Lancaster, Bailrigg House,
Lancaster, by 23rd September, 1964.

Members of the congregation are respectfully requested to be seated by 10-20 a.m. at the latest.

UNIVERSITY OF LANCASTER INVITATION 1964
ZZZ00465 (Reproduced by kind permission of Lancaster Library)

would be prepared to give up the Bailrigg estate. Fortunately Mr Barton-Townley was a believer in Lancaster's case for a university, and the family were prepared to sell for £50,000.

The voting was overwhelmingly in favour of Lancaster. On 23 November 1961 it was announced in the House of Commons by Henry Brooke, Chief Secretary to the Treasury, that 'the Government has accepted the advice of the University Grants Committee that the fourth new university should be established at Lancaster'. Following on from the decision, the land at Bailrigg was purchased by the City Council for letting on a long lease to the university. Bailrigg House itself was to be retained for university use. However, Lancaster University itself came into existence before its buildings. Lancaster City Council purchased the old Waring & Gillow factory (left) and spent over £200,000 on converting, equipping and furnishing it. On 9 October 1964 a service was held at Lancaster Priory Church for the inauguration of the first academic

THE FORMER WARING AND GILLOW FACTORY ON ST LEONARDGATE 2004 L10720k (Robert Swain)

Seating Reservation in the
Ashton Hall of the Town Hall, Lancaster

THE UNIVER

GROUND FLOOR L 24

CONGREGATION

for the

INSTALLATION

of

HER ROYAL HIGHNESS PRINCESS ALEXANDRA

The Honourable Mrs. Angus Ogilvy

as

FIRST CHANCELLOR OF THE UNIVERSITY

and for the

CONFERMENT OF HONORARY DEGREES

UNIVERSITY OF LANCASTER, INSTALLATION OF THE CHANCELLOR 1964 ZZZ00464

THE UNIVERSITY OF LANCASTER

LUNCHEON

on the occasion of the

Installation of the First Chancellor

Her Royal Highness Princess Alexandra

The Honourable Mrs. Angus Ogilvy

———

Grand Ballroom
of the Winter Gardens, Morecambe

———

Wednesday November 18th 1964

UNIVERSITY OF LANCASTER, INSTALLATION OF THE CHANCELLOR 1964 ZZZ00468

---

session of the University of Lancaster and St Martin's College of Education, Lancaster. On 18 November Princess Alexandra was installed as the first Chancellor, a post she held for forty years. The installation and the conferment of honorary degrees took place in the Ashton Hall of Lancaster Town Hall; many Lancastrians turned out to watch the princess's arrival. On its opening, the university had 13 professors, 32 teaching staff and 8 library staff.

More space became needed, and other buildings were rented from Lancaster City Council, including Centenary House (a former Congregational church, now The Friary), and a quiet study in Great John Street.

Work commenced on the premises at Bailrigg. The university campus was to centre round Alexandra Square, built above the underpass. This was dug down so as to allow for double-decker buses to pass through, and two flights of steps led from the stops up into the square.

The university itself was to be laid out in lines from Alexandra Square, North Spine and South Spine, and these and other walkways were to have cover from the rain. Also, this design would allow for future expansion to be simply added on. The boiler-house chimney had to be 125 feet high to satisfy regulations, but it needed to be disguised, so Bowland Tower was built around it, adding an interesting feature to the design of the university as a whole.

UNIVERSITY OF LANCASTER, BOWLAND TOWER 2004
L10721k (Robert Swain)

**UNIVERSITY OF LANCASTER, THE CHAPLAINCY
CENTRE 2004** L10722k (Robert Swain)

Close to the Square was the Computer Building, housing a large computer in an air-conditioned room. It was operated by punched tape. Now, there are dozens of computers in the library alone. The Chaplaincy Centre (above), built on a trefoil design, needed careful consideration so that no one denomination dominated and all could share. As a symbol of this ecumenicalism, on top of the building there is one spike and two crosses, and these form the basis of the university logo.

In its early years in particular, the university had a radical reputation; in 1965 there were protests about American involvement in Vietnam, and in the 1970s a lecturer, David Craig, was dismissed following an argument about freedom of speech. This attitude led to a rather uneasy relationship between the local people and the students.

A major development was the Centre for North West Regional Studies, which was founded in 1973 to help researchers with work on north-west projects. Now, there is a degree course on Lake District studies. The library was extended in 1977, and provides very useful facilities for local people engaged in research work. Princess Alexandra opened the Ruskin Library, which is devoted to the works of John Ruskin, in 1998.

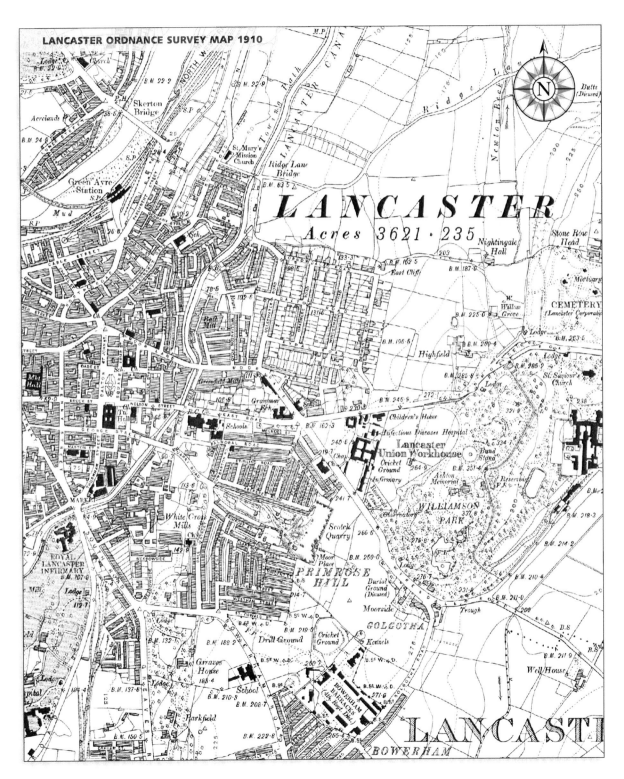

LANCASTER ORDNANCE SURVEY MAP 1910

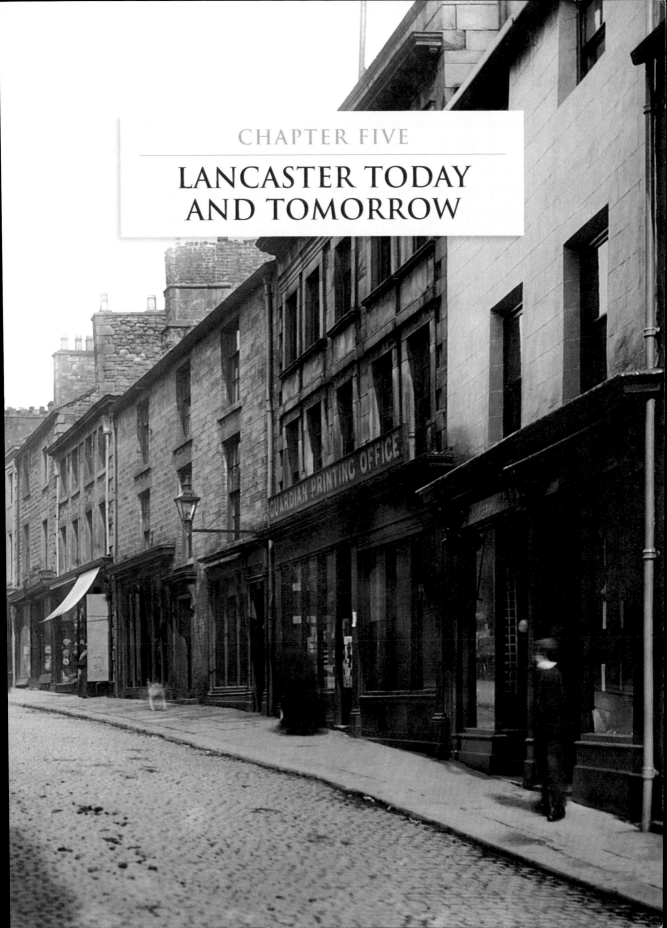

LANCASTER has lost most of its manufacturing industry, but it still has a lot going for it. As manufacturing declined, the university, together with St Martin's College, developed. The university is growing ever nearer to Galgate, causing some criticism that there will soon be no green space between the two. However, its expansion does provide work locally in a variety of ways. Accommodation for the people working at both the university and the college has to be provided, and many local people are employed on the sites.

Not only are there facilities for the younger students, but there is also much on offer for those who are older. Various courses are run (during vacations as well) that are of interest to older people; the Department of Continuing Education was founded in 1981. Also, the university provides research facilities for those living locally and working on projects of their own. Access is very easy, as everything is on one main site. Many buses run between Morecambe, Lancaster and the university, passing St Martin's College (now part of the new University of Cumbria) on the way, providing ease of access between all of them.

In 2001 the modern new bus station was opened. It has a fully covered hall, so that passengers no longer have to stand outside on cold, windy days, perhaps also getting wet as well.

BOWERHAM BARRACKS, THE KEEP 2004 L10723k (Robert Swain)

The keep of the former Bowerham Barracks is now a part of St Martin's College, and so are the other former military buildings.

THE MILLENNIUM BRIDGE OVER THE LUNE 2004 L10725k (Robert Swain)

Whilst there is now no manufacturing at White Cross, several businesses are run from there, and also adult further education covering a wide variety of subjects is based there. The site is run by Lancashire Enterprises.

The Millennium Bridge spanning the River Lune was opened in March 2001, providing pedestrian and cycling routes across the river both for local people and tourists. The bridge is based on a picture of a sailing ship in the nearby Maritime Museum. It links the two parts of the Riverside Park, a walk and cycleway between Morecambe and Caton.

New developments in the town are now designed to try to be in keeping with its general appearance. For example, Charter House in Dalton Square (page 112), the home of the local Inland Revenue office, was built to be externally in keeping with its Georgian neighbours. The Inland Revenue have occupied various buildings in Lancaster, and were split into sections. In 1961 the Employments Section was based in Cable Street.

THE BUS STATION 2004 L10724k (Robert Swain)

WILLIAMSON PARK 1912 64219p

Today, the fountain is in a different place and the trees and bushes have grown. This picture was taken near the bridge, but the rhododendron on the left now obscures the view.

CHARTER HOUSE, DALTON SQUARE 2004 L10726k (Robert Swain)

Anybody with the slightest interest in history can spend many hours visiting the various museums, including the Judges'

INLAND REVENUE ENVELOPE 1961 ZZZ00462

Lodgings and the Cottage Museum, as well as the City Museum and the Maritime Museum. Lancaster Castle and the Priory Church are open to visitors, and draw in many people. Tourism now has quite a large role to play in Lancaster, and it will no doubt expand. Not only are there the historical attractions mentioned above, but there are also Williamson Park and the Lancaster Canal.

The park had become rather run down, particularly around the water features. Lottery grants have led to their restoration, including the fountain and an artificial waterfall tumbling down a rock face. The Temple Shelter had long gone, but it too has been restored. Further land that was part of the

Moor Hospital, formerly the old County Asylum (which closed over a period up to 2000 following changes in the care of the mentally impaired), has been added to the park.

During the summer season, plays are performed out in the open, often plays by Shakespeare, but sometimes by others, such as a dramatisation of Chaucer's 'Canterbury Tales'. Those performances are seasonal, but year-round plays, and a variety of other entertainments, are put on regularly both by professionals and amateurs at the Duke's Playhouse, which is housed in the former St Anne's Church, and in the Grand Theatre.

In the town centre are the various shops; William Stout, the ironmonger and grocer we met in Chapter Two, might well still feel at home here. After many years of the open-air market only selling fruit, vegetables and other produce in Church Street on a Saturday, with some stalls on a Wednesday, the market has returned to Market Square. There are some stalls on Cheapside as well, and a wide variety of goods and produce are now sold there.

The Millennium Ribble Link at Preston has joined the Lancaster Canal to the main system to the first time, so that boats can sail to the town from other areas. Near the city is the seaside resort of Morecambe, and there is much magnificent countryside to explore. Some of this can be seen by following the Millennium Park from the Millennium Bridge or various other access points, passing up or down by the Lune.

Lancaster is not a place to by-pass on the motorway or dash through on the way to somewhere else. It has much to offer local people and visitors alike. In many ways, its past could be said to be its future.

THE FOUNTAIN, WILLIAMSON PARK 2004
L10727k (Robert Swain)

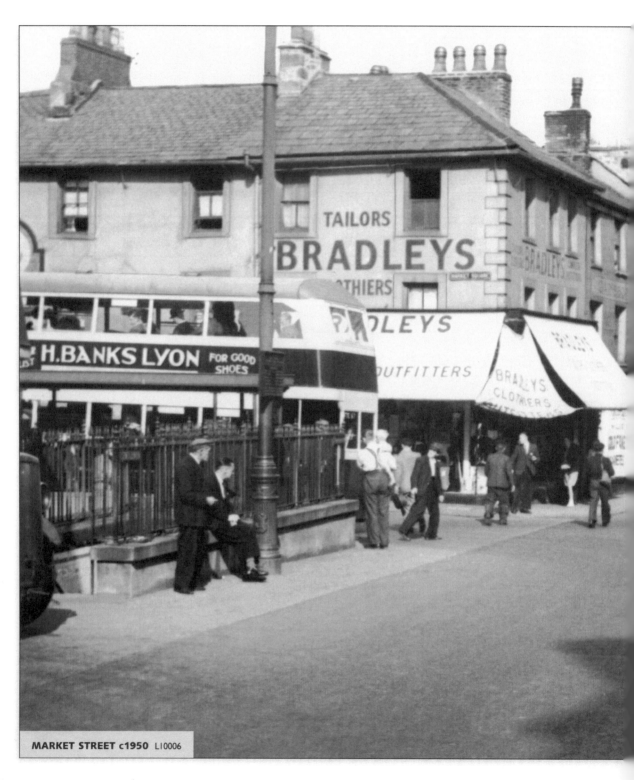

MARKET STREET c1950 LI0006

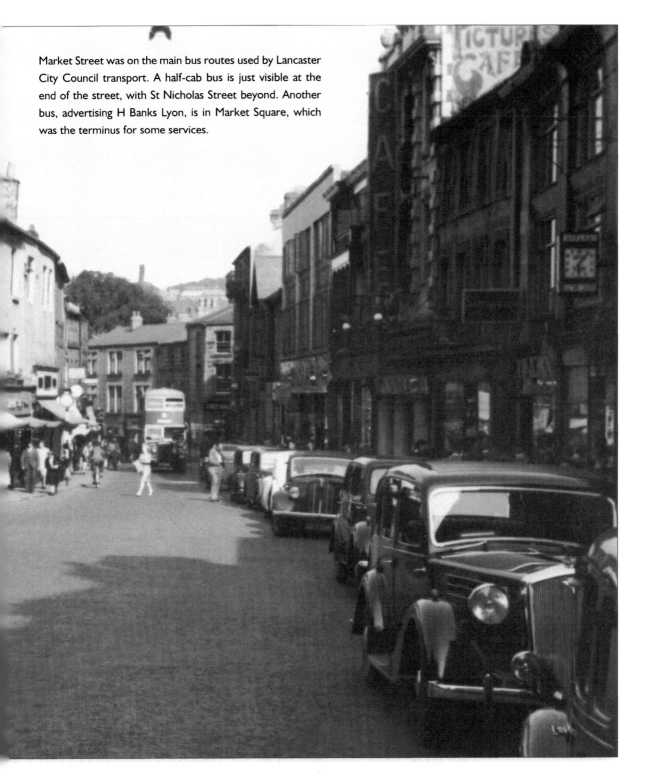

Market Street was on the main bus routes used by Lancaster City Council transport. A half-cab bus is just visible at the end of the street, with St Nicholas Street beyond. Another bus, advertising H Banks Lyon, is in Market Square, which was the terminus for some services.

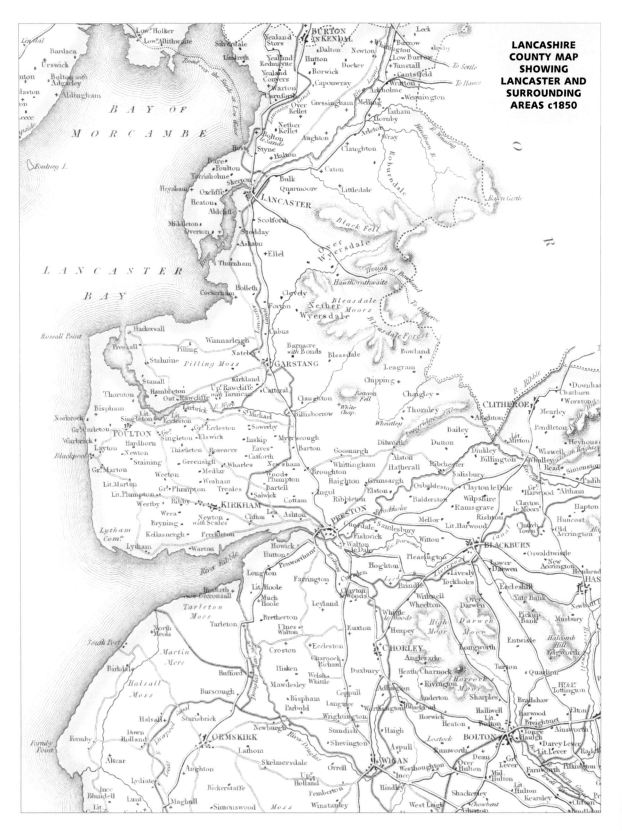

LANCASHIRE
COUNTY MAP
SHOWING
LANCASTER AND
SURROUNDING
AREAS c1850

116

ACKNOWLEDGEMENT

The author gratefully acknowledges the assistance of Lancaster Reference Library and Lancaster City Council in providing material and information for use in this book.

BIBLIOGRAPHY

Lancaster City Museums have published leaflets on several aspects of the history of the town, and these can be purchased at the City and Maritime Museums.

Lancaster, a History Andrew White.

A History of Lancaster 1193-1993 Edited Andrew White.

Lancaster Priory The official guide to be purchased there.

A Walker's Guide to the Lancaster Canal Robert Swain.

Town Maps of old Lancaster

The Buildings of Georgian Lancaster Andrew White.

Victorian Terraced Houes in Lancaster Andrew White and Michael Winstanley.

The Lino King. The Life and Times of Lord Ashton Sus Ashworth.

Lancaster Guardian Several editions were consulted in the writing of this book.

FRITH PRODUCTS & SERVICES

Francis Frith would doubtless be pleased to know that the pioneering publishing venture he started in 1860 still continues today. Over a hundred and forty years later, The Francis Frith Collection continues in the same innovative tradition and is now one of the foremost publishers of vintage photographs in the world. Some of the current activities include:

INTERIOR DECORATION

Today Frith's photographs can be seen framed and as giant wall murals in thousands of pubs, restaurants, hotels, banks, retail stores and other public buildings throughout the country. In every case they enhance the unique local atmosphere of the places they depict and provide reminders of gentler days in an increasingly busy and frenetic world.

PRODUCT PROMOTIONS

Frith products are used by many major companies to promote the sales of their own products or to reinforce their own history and heritage. Frith promotions have been used by Hovis bread, Courage beers, Scots Porage Oats, Colman's mustard, Cadbury's foods, Mellow Birds coffee, Dunhill pipe tobacco, Guinness, and Bulmer's Cider.

GENEALOGY AND FAMILY HISTORY

As the interest in family history and roots grows world-wide, more and more people are turning to Frith's photographs of Great Britain for images of the towns, villages and streets where their ancestors lived; and, of course, photographs of the churches and chapels where their ancestors were christened, married and buried are an essential part of every genealogy tree and family album.

FRITH PRODUCTS

All Frith photographs are available Framed or just as Mounted Prints and Posters (size 23 x 16 inches). These may be ordered from the address below. Other products available are - Address Books, Calendars, Jigsaws, Canvas Prints, Postcards and local and prestige books.

THE INTERNET

Already ninety thousand Frith photographs can be viewed and purchased on the internet through the Frith websites and a myriad of partner sites.

For more detailed information on Frith products, look at this site:
www.francisfrith.com

See the complete list of Frith Books at: www.francisfrith.com
This web site is regularly updated with the latest list of publications from The Francis Frith Collection. If you wish to buy books relating to another part of the country that your local bookshop does not stock, you may purchase on-line.

For further information, trade, or author enquiries please contact us at the address below:
The Francis Frith Collection, Unit 6, Oakley Business Park, Wylye Road, Dinton, Wiltshire SP3 5EU.
Tel: +44 (0)1722 716 376 Fax: +44 (0)1722 716 881 Email: sales@francisfrith.co.uk

See Frith products on the internet at www.francisfrith.com

FREE PRINT OF YOUR CHOICE
CHOOSE A PHOTOGRAPH FROM THIS BOOK
+ £3.80 POSTAGE

Mounted Print
Overall size 14 x 11 inches (355 x 280mm)

TO RECEIVE YOUR FREE PRINT

Choose any Frith photograph in this book

Simply complete the Voucher opposite and return it with your remittance for £3.50 (to cover postage and handling) and we will print the photograph of your choice in SEPIA (size 11 x 8 inches) and supply it in a cream mount ready to frame (overall size 14 x 11 inches).

Order additional Mounted Prints
at HALF PRICE - £12.00 each (normally £24.00)

If you would like to order more Frith prints from this book, possibly as gifts for friends and family, you can buy them at half price (with no additional postage costs).

Have your Mounted Prints framed

For an extra £20.00 per print you can have your mounted print(s) framed in an elegant polished wood and gilt moulding, overall size 16 x 13 inches (no additional postage required).

IMPORTANT!

❶ Please note: aerial photographs and photographs with a reference number starting with a "Z" are not Frith photographs and cannot be supplied under this offer.

❷ Offer valid for delivery to one UK address only.

❸ These special prices are only available if you use this form to order. You must use the ORIGINAL VOUCHER on this page (no copies permitted). We can only despatch to one UK address.

❹ This offer cannot be combined with any other offer.

As a customer your name & address will be stored by Frith but not sold or rented to third parties. Your data will be used for the purpose of this promotion only.

Send completed Voucher form to:

**The Francis Frith Collection,
19 Kingsmead Business Park, Gillingham,
Dorset SP8 5FB**

Voucher for *FREE* and *Reduced Price Frith Prints*

Please do not photocopy this voucher. Only the original is valid, so please fill it in, cut it out and return it to us with your order.

Picture ref no	Page no	Qty	Mounted @ £12.00	Framed + £20.00	Total Cost £
		1	Free of charge*	£	£
			£12.00	£	£
			£12.00	£	£
			£12.00	£	£
			£12.00	£	£
			£12.00	£	£

Please allow 28 days for delivery. Offer available to one UK address only

* Post & handling		£3.80
Total Order Cost		**£**

Title of this book . . . .

I enclose a cheque/postal order for £ . . . .
made payable to 'The Francis Frith Collection'

OR please debit my Mastercard / Visa / Maestro card, details below

Card Number:

Issue No (Maestro only):   Valid from (Maestro):

Card Security Number: Expires:

Signature:

Name Mr/Mrs/Ms ....

Address ....

....

....

.... Postcode ....

Daytime Tel No ....

Email ....

Valid to 31/12/16

Can you help us with information about any of the Frith photographs in this book?

We are gradually compiling an historical record for each of the photographs in the Frith archive. It is always fascinating to find out the names of the people shown in the pictures, as well as insights into the shops, buildings and other features depicted.

If you recognize anyone in the photographs in this book, or if you have information not already included in the author's caption, do let us know. We would love to hear from you, and will try to publish it in future books or articles.

An Invitation from The Francis Frith Collection to Share Your Memories

The 'Share Your Memories' feature of our website allows members of the public to add personal memories relating to the places featured in our photographs, or comment on others already added. Seeing a place from your past can rekindle forgotten or long held memories. Why not visit the website, find photographs of places you know well and add YOUR story for others to read and enjoy? We would love to hear from you!

www.francisfrith.com/memories

Our production team

Frith books are produced by a small dedicated team at offices near Salisbury. Most have worked with the Frith Collection for many years. All have in common one quality: they have a passion for the Frith Collection.

Frith Books and Gifts

We have a wide range of books and gifts available on our website utilising our photographic archive, many of which can be individually personalised.

www.francisfrith.com